BREAKING AND SCHOOLING

BREAKING AND SCHOOLING

AND

OTHER HORSE KNOWLEDGE
PRACTISED AND PROVED

BY

MAJOR H. FAUDEL-PHILLIPS

J. A. ALLEN & CO.,
1 LOWER GROSVENOR PLACE, LONDON, S.W.1.

*Originally published
as*
"Horse Knowledge Practised and Proved"

© 1962, J. A. ALLEN & CO. LTD.

First published in this edition 1973

Reprinted 1975

SBN 85131 185 7

*Printed in Great Britain by
Lewis Reprints Ltd.
member of Brown Knight & Truscott Group
London and Tonbridge*

CONTENTS

	PAGE
FOREWORD	9

CHAPTER

I.	LONG REIN DRIVING	15
II.	MOUTHING	26
III.	BITTING	36
IV.	BREAKING AND TRAINING, UP TO THREE YEARS OLD	47
V.	BACKING AND RIDING A COLT, AND RE-TRAINING OF OTHER HORSES	53
VI.	STABLE MANAGEMENT	68
VII.	SADDLERY	81
VIII.	SHOWING	88
IX.	CHILDREN'S PONIES	99

Contents

CHAPTER		PAGE
X.	When Buying a Horse—A Few Things to Remember	107
XI.	Riding Kit—How to Dress	116
XII.	Miscellaneous Do's and Don't's	121

Foreword

In the following chapters I have tried to put down as shortly and concisely as possible some of the things I have learned about the breaking and training of horses and matters appertaining thereto.

In my opinion it is impossible to make hard and fast rules and so I am only going to try to tell you what I found useful, therefore, if any of " the heads " or anyone who " knows it all " should pick up this little book, I ask them to remember that it is not written for them, but rather to try to help those who wish to know how to break a youngster and make him into a comfortable ride quickly and cheaply.

If I require an introduction to my readers, may I say, without boasting, that I was never afraid of one I had trained letting me down by his ride, whether in the Show Ring, in Hunting, or in playing Polo.

I am going to try to tell you my methods but you must use your own personality and judgment in applying same. I know that when in a tight place with a youngster playing up, or in a Championship, when every ounce had to be produced, I never took my eyes off my horse's ears. Concentration helps no end in everything.

To try to lay down hard and fast rules such as I have read in books, or do this and do that, is not always possible, horses vary so much, but if you are in sympathy with your mount, and he has some confidence in you, you have at any rate a good basis to work on, because, mind you, this bad temper, nappiness, etc., we hear so much of, is more often than not nerves (in exactly the same way that a dog often fights purely because he is nervous). Many a time if you would drop your hand and sit still instead of raising your voice and stick, and give a soft whistle, the trouble would not happen and he would go quietly on.

I have tried to tell my experience in training and breaking, from foals onward. Also for what I have termed re-training—which is perhaps more important, as so many people buy who cannot afford to breed horses, or who do not want to be bothered with all their baby troubles, and the years of waiting.

No apology is made for the English or grammar in this book. I am not an author, but an ordinary person who, amongst other things, won the Richmond Hack Championship seven times in all (three times outright) trying to pass on to anyone who may find it useful, for a few shillings, knowledge that cost me a great deal of money, time and trouble, not

FOREWORD

only to acquire but to put into action and prove at any rate to my own satisfaction.

In my opinion the early training of all saddle horses and ponies is the same, remember I am not including race horses of any size, sort, or description, I know nothing about them; but simply Hunters, Hacks, and Polo Ponies, for which all the groundwork and early training is the same, when you are working to try to obtain as near as can be a perfect ride.

Bitting is a difficult thing to write about, because a bitting expert is born, not made. Perhaps I may class myself as one, for many times it has come to me in the night what to put on such and such a horse in the morning to stop his doing some little thing which was not quite right.

Stable management largely depends on one's means and the local conditions.

I have put in a few words about kit, saddlery, etc., because of the things one has seen and cannot help feeling certain would not have seen if the person had had some way of finding out how to present themselves and their steed. You know what I mean: a hunting stock like a poultice round the throat, a so-called hunting crop (held upside down) and a kind of white web hunting breastplate or martingale. Sort of things that either singly or combined do not belong to the horse world. I hope these chapters will penetrate to the purveyors of these articles. They probably think they are right in selling them, but I would dearly love to save some of these people from buying such things and advertising the fact that they do not know; when a sixpenny stick, a collar and tie, and a leather martingale need never be out of place, even when hunting.

My few odd points on buying a horse are only suggestions, but may help someone when that awful moment arrives and you go into a dealer's yard and the great man produces the very article, fast enough to win a race, clever enough to climb a tree, and " 'is manners are such, Sir, lord, 'e could sit down to dinner and be'ave 'isself like a perfect gent." In the face of this eulogy on the steed every idea leaves us, and we are afraid to tell the great man that we do not like the three-cornered brute, in case he asks us why.

Perhaps if you can throw your mind back to one or two of my little points it will save you from buying one you do not really want, or on the other hand make you buy one who is not looking quite his best at the moment you see him. The former you will find out for certain, the latter you may not, unless you see someone who has bought him sailing over a country ahead of you, or having a topping ride while you are having your teeth shaken at every stride.

You may wonder why I am suddenly

FOREWORD

blossoming forth into print. I will explain to you.

In 1926, when I was living in the South of France there came seven gallant soldier men to jump at the Horse Show at Nice. I was enormously interested to find that they were as keen as I myself have always been on what I call a finished horse.

Happening to come into contact with them a great deal, and knowing the ropes, I was able to get things for them and their horses which otherwise they might not have easily obtained.

It was therefore my privelege to be there when they were schooling in the early morning, and I soon discovered that the hack man and the jumping man were getting together at last, in fact, that my pet theory was coming into being. That is to say, that a perfectly broken and balanced horse is what is required, be it for Show Jumping, Hunting, Hacking, and, needless to say, Polo.

The leader of these seven gallant soldier men asked me one day if I would tell them some of the things I used to do when breaking my horses, so we had a few minutes together in their stable yard, and I found that it lay in my power to tell them a good many things that would be of great use to them, not only in training their jumpers, but in teaching and training their men and horses, on their return to England. Later it occurred to me that

I might be able to help other people in the same way if I committed to paper a few of the theories I had worked out and proved ; hence this book.

HORSE KNOWLEDGE
PRACTISED AND PROVED

CHAPTER I

LONG REIN DRIVING

A person who has studied the use of the long reins can get a colt a very long way on the road to being broken before he is backed. Long rein driving is not easy, and some people may find it tedious, but it is not difficult if you stop to consider for a moment the action of your reins. I am going to deal with the whole question of long rein driving, that is to say, the driving of unbroken colts, or the re-making of a horse that has been spoilt, under one section.

Web Reins. The first thing to consider is the reins; use web reins, not too heavy, because of the weight when they get wet, and not too light or you cannot hold them, and they cut your hands to pieces, therefore a nice medium web with a leather billet at each end on a swivel ring is recommended. You may not understand this swivel ring, but any saddler will show you and the reason for it; which is to prevent the reins from twisting. A buckle in the middle is essential, but beware of this buckle when running the reins quickly through your hands.

Cord Reins. You can of course use cord reins ; for web ones are expensive, but they last much longer, and cord when it is wet is so frightfully difficult to deal with, it gets so kinked and hard. By the way, do you know how to untangle a kinked cord ? Use a broom handle or a fixed bar of any sort, take one turn of the cord round it, and pull on the end you have put round. Now having got your reins, let us consider the rest of the paraphernalia required ; it is very simple ; the first and most important thing is a big strong stable head collar (in the case of an aged horse I put this stable head collar on over a snaffle bridle, with a straight barred snaffle for choice, with no reins and no nose band), a good strong roller, a piece of cord about six feet long and a short piece of cord about a foot long, or a short strap and a ring.

Now that all sounds very complicated, but let me just explain it to you. In the case of your aged horse, or even a three-year-old, who is ready for a bit, take your short piece of cord, tie it on to one of the rings of the bit, pass it through the ring I told you to get, and tie it to the other ring of the bit. This leaves your ring free, running from side to side, along your piece of cord.

Check Rein. Now put on your roller. I am taking it for granted that we are dealing with a horse who has had a roller on, otherwise the question is dealt with elsewhere. Attach your long piece of cord to the side of your roller ; bring the end through the ring that is running on the short piece of cord, and attach it to the other side of your roller, to the length you may require ; tie the cord on your roller, so that it is at a nice level, neither too high nor too low. Now what have you got ? A nice check rein to keep your horse from raking about too much, but at the same time, owing to the ring, he has perfect freedom to turn his head from side to side. This is a very good check rein to be used at any time. I very often use it when mouthing in the stable (see Mouthing), attaching the ring to the head collar instead of the bit.

Secret of Perfect Mouth. You are now ready to put your reins on, buckle your billets into the " D " each side of your stable head collar, because here, dear reader, is my pet theory, and here lies the secret of making the horse with a perfect mouth ; you are going to drive him off his nose. I know with a big awkward horse it is a difficult thing to do at first ; but before going any further we will consider the action of the reins.

You will start on a circle ; you are unlikely to have a school, you are unlikely even to have a yard where you can drive ; well, then, my advice is, go into the corner of a field where you get a certain amount of support from the angle of a hedge, or of a post and rails.

Action of Reins. Now as to the action of

these reins; the inner rein leads and keeps him on the circle, your outer rein, round his quarters, keeps those hind quarters from flying out, your inner rein will be the tightest, because you must leave a certain amount of room for the action of his outer hind leg as he moves round on the circle.

What effect is that action having on your stable head collar ? A sawing action of the nose band. It is a give and take motion; and what is the result ? The bridge of his nose gets sore, and before very long he comes to your hand. " Oh, how cruel; the poor horse has got a sore place on his nose ! " I will deal with the healing of that in a minute, but now think of what would happen to the bars of that horse's mouth if you had buckled those billets to the rings of any bit. Any and everybody can see the sore on the bridge of the nose, nobody, except somebody looking for it, can see the dreadful condition of that horse's mouth.

In the old schools a Cavesson bridle was used; a big thing strapped round his face with a ring in the centre of his nose, to which was attached a single rein. He was belted round in a circle with his quarters flying anywhere, and to change him and go the other way, he had to be hauled in, and started off again. However, I consider that even this was a better method than driving on the bars of the mouth, and I hope you will give my method a trial, and reap from your trial the same benefit that I did when long rein driving in this way.

Commencing Operations. Having got your horse into the corner where you intend to commence operations, if you have somebody to help you, let him be quietly led round in a circle. In the case of a three-year-old or a baby, for the first minute or two, have your outside rein over his back or neck, wherever it lies, and let him be led round you. If you have not anybody to help you, then lead him round yourself, gradually getting further away from him. Concentrate the whole of your attention on your inner rein, and when you have got a little way from him, get out to the full length of your rein or you may get kicked, and hang on. Let him do whatever he likes, plant your feet and hang on to that inner rein; when he has had his buck and kick, turn him round as best you can, and get him on the other rein. Let him have a belt round that way. That will take the edge off his freshness, especially if your field is a little bit deep.

Rein Round Quarters. Now get your outer rein round his quarters, leave it fairly loose, let him have his kick out as much as ever he wants to, all the better if he kicks it up under his tail; let him kick on till he finds it does not hurt him, but if he looks like doing any damage, you can stop him by a series of hearty jerks on the inner rein ; you are only jerking his nose.

We will now take it that we have got over his first ticklishness, and that you have got your horse going quietly round on his circle.

Human Voice. I wish now to say something about the word of command, because a human voice is such a tremendous factor in horse training. If you can school yourself never to use the word " Whoa," except sharply, to mean " Halt," you will have acquired one very good habit. You can get your horse so trained on the long reins to " Whoa " that when you are riding him it is like pressing a button. Your next word is " Back " (later I indicate the system of teaching him to back), but you will get him so that when you say " Whoa," he will stop ; " Back " (not sharply, but a little drawled), he will stop and take a step or two back.

Another good tip. I always used " Up," to start a horse off, saying it gently when I wanted him to move off into a walk, and sharp and loud when I wanted him to jump into a canter. The fourth and last word is " Change " ; when I changed a horse on the circle, when driving him, be it at the walk, trot, or canter, I always said " Change."

Change. I generally used the word " Steady " as a prefix to all these words, so that he knew something was coming. We have now got our horse going round on the

LONG REIN DRIVING 21

circle, and we want to change him to go the other way. Well, at first you do this from a walk, stopping him—you stop him by an equal pressure on both reins—and then to change him you start him off again, tightening the outer rein and letting out the inner rein, gradually working him up to do this at any pace.

Back. Next comes teaching him to "Back." If you have not taught him to back as a baby (see chapter on Youngsters) you will want somebody to help you; give that person a little bit of stick, get behind your horse with your reins and say "Back"; he will probably resist at first; if so, make up your mind which front foot you wish him to move first, then try again, pulling a little bit more on that rein, and, of course, saying "Back." If he still resists, let your assistant tread lightly on his coronet, or just tap him lightly on the shin bone with a little stick; do not haul and tear at him, he is not being pig-headed, he does not understand, and I want him to come to it easily and quickly, otherwise, you will get him backing with his head too low, and once he gets into this habit, you will have to re-teach him when you get on his back.

Be careful when you start him forward, with "Up," and a flick of the rein on the side, you yourself being prepared at once to jump on one side or the other, and circle him, because, unless you are a giant, you cannot hold a horse standing behind him if he makes a spring straight forward.

Now, by getting him to work on these lines, you can run about the field with him on long reins, doing anything you like.

The Nose. Let us next deal with that sore nose ; when you get him in bathe it, and put some boric ointment on it, or anything healing. I am afraid the next morning you will have to take him out and make him sore again, but put in your pocket a piece of felt, about three inches wide and six inches long, with two tapes sewn on the back of it, about four inches apart, leaving the ends as ties. If, when his first buck is over, and you have put him through what he learnt the day before, he settles down quietly, take your piece of felt and put it inside his nose band, attaching it to same with the tapes. If you cannot hold him, you must take it off again ; but after a few days he will work entirely with this felt, and never have another sore.

Straight Driving. When you have got your horse thoroughly broken on the long reins so that you have control of him, then take him for walks each day for a few minutes ; before you go back to the stable, drive him straight in front of you. This teaches him to walk away by himself, and to walk straight.

Knee Caps. If you are going to walk him anywhere, or work him where the ground is hard, or on a road, always put on knee caps ;

Long Rein Driving

for a bird may fly out of the hedge, he is startled, and crosses his legs, down he goes, and your beautiful horse is ruined. The fitting of knee caps : strap them on tight two inches above the knee, then slip them down the knee. This should be just right, not too tight ; never strap a knee cap into the position you are going to use it, or it will be too tight. The bottom straps should be absolutely loose ; they are only to prevent flapping up.

When you are long rein driving, never stop because a horse gets his leg over the rein ; it is generally the hind leg over the outside rein ; ease that rein so as not to cause a rub, and let him carry on. If he kicks at it, it does not matter ; let him think, whatever happens, that nothing is wrong, and in after life if he gets his leg over a trace, or a bar, or if he gets tied up with his bridle after a fall out hunting, or tied up in any way, he will not be frightened.

Loosing Horse. If you have a yard, or any place where he will not hurt himself, let him loose, with his long reins trailing, let him tear round ; stand in the middle and light your pipe ; when you are ready, and he has stopped, walk up to him and pick up the end of the long reins, never mind how they are, let him walk on round as though nothing had happened, then throw them down again and go away and leave him for a minute or two ; come back again, and walk up to him and pat him if he will let you, if he will not, pick up the end of the long reins and bring him to you, and give him a bit of tobacco, or grass, and let him go again.

It is a strange thing that the majority of horses lose their nerves when they find themselves loose, but if you train them like this, they are quite accustomed to it and they are not frightened.

The Passage. You can teach a horse to "passage," either way, on the long reins, by leading with the inner rein, and supporting with the outer. You must get pretty square with him to do this at the start, but afterwards you can do it from behind. The "passage," brother beginner, is a horse moving crabwise, or sideways, crossing his near fore and his near hind legs over his off fore and his off hind legs or vice versa.

The Inspector General of Cavalry was inspecting a crack regiment one day, and a subaltern was told to drill his troop in the riding school; he was one of those good old-fashioned subalterns, whose horses looked well and whose men adored him; could ride top of a hunt, and a good polo player, but had not a great knowledge of the cavalry drill book. He was called out to the middle of the school, and told to give the detail of the "passage": he soon got tied up, and jumping off his horse, got down on all fours in the tan, saying: "Oh, dash it, this is what I mean," crossing his left hand and his left foot over his

Long Rein Driving

right hand and his right foot. Rumour has it that he shortly afterwards turned his sword into a ploughshare.

By the time I had finished a colt's long rein education, he would go anywhere and fear nothing. I used to tie tins, handkerchiefs, cloths, and other things, all over him, and after the first couple of times he did not mind anything. I used to throw down white rags and pieces of corrugated iron, with stones and bits of iron to rattle on them, and teach him to walk over them, first by following me, then, when he had found out that they were not going to hurt him, to go in front of me, on the long reins.

Confidence. A horse is like a child; you can teach him to have implicit confidence in you and thus to have confidence in himself. I was teaching a little chap to ride one day, when he suddenly slipped over sideways, and hung by his stirrup. I said "Whoa," the pony stood stock still (he was used to having things hung round him). I put the little chap up again, and said, "That is a new method of riding that I do not know," and he went on with his lesson without the least idea of the danger he had been in. Think what the result might have been had it not been a perfectly trained pony. That, my reader, is long rein driving, and can be achieved, and your animal still have a virgin mouth.

CHAPTER II

MOUTHING

This chapter is the result of years of study, thought, and experiment, and what is written herein may help the most knowledgable to deal with an awkward mouth; for two heads are better than one.

I believe that no such thing as a bad mouthed horse was ever foaled, and I further believe that no one-sided mouthed horse was ever foaled.

It is my conviction that hard mouths, one-sided mouths, and the majority of horses that bolt, and horses that nap, are made by mutton-fisted men and women, and that all these things originate from pain, and fear of pain.

Yes, it is a sweeping assertion, I know, but I have stated my belief, and in this chapter hope to try and help you, first: to make good mouths on your young horses, and second: to re-make the mouths of horses you buy, that have hard mouths, or pull, etc.

You can! I assure you it can be done. I have done it, not once, but many times; not always, but often. One horse I bought,

128 guineas, at the Lane (yes, that made the boys stare); he had only one side to his mouth, I got him to ride comfortably, but I never cured him, though I got him to drop his head when you touched his bad side.

Action of Curb Bridle. Have you ever seriously thought, for a few minutes, of the action of a double bridle, or any curb bit? If not, please do. What is it? A leverage, is it not? From the bottom of the bit, where the rein is attached to the top of the head, with a downward pressure of the mouthpiece on the bars of the mouth, and an upward pressure of curb chain, behind the jaw; in some bridles pinching the flesh at the corners of the mouth, between bit and chain. (More of this later.)

Well now; think what that must mean to a horse, when you see the way some people, I regret to say, many people, catch hold of them.

Position of Hands. The first thing to alleviate this is to get the hands in the right position. May I quote the words of the old Cavalry drill book: " Wrists rounded, thumbs across the body," and I add to these words: " elbows lightly touching the sides."

Now, please put your book down—Elbows just touching your sides, wrists rounded, thumbs across the body, back of the hand to the front. Then work your hands backwards and forwards, from the wrists, keep your elbows in ; now, do you see the play you can thus give to your horse's mouth ?

Stop a moment, with your fingers closed, knuckles to the front, wrists straight. A straight pull, is it not ? No play, or your fingers down, back of the hand up, straight pull, no play ; well, that's one of the first things, and keep your elbows comfortably in, or you lose the benefit of rounded wrists.

Mouthing the Colt. First of all we will talk about the untouched mouth of a colt, about one of the most interesting parts of making and breaking, and if I muddle the start up a bit with my chapter on Long Rein Driving, you must forgive me.

The first thing is to get the young animal accustomed to something in his mouth, without the least chance of it hurting him or bearing on the bars of the mouth. The best thing for this is a nice light curb chain and two pieces of string, or two supple straps (string for choice) to attach to the stable head collar.

Curb Chains for Mouthing. Curb chains for mouthing, re-mouthing, and keeping all mouths fresh, was one of my greatest assets, or shall I say secrets. One curb chain for a yearling or two-year-old, two are enough for a three-year-old, and three should suffice anything else ; but on an old dry mouthed hunter, I have used five, before I got him champing, and myself happy.

Attaching Single Chain to Head Collar.
The method of attaching the chains to the stable head collar is simple, but very important. In the case of the single chain, attach a string to each end, and bring them up under the head collar, inside the nose band, and tie them inside the loop of the brow band, or if you have a stable head collar with a ring where the head-piece joins the cheek-piece, attach them to it. Why not attach it to the nose band, you say; because if you are leading your animal you will interfere with his mouth, and if he is on the pillar reins, for the same reason. If he is loose in his box he cannot interfere with it by rubbing, or get caught up on the door or anything.

String inside Nose Band. For the same reason, you put your string or strap inside the nose-band, and up inside the head collar, also in that way you get a beautiful straight fall, and no chance of pressure on the mouth.

Attaching Two or more Curb Chains.
To attach two or more curb chains, tie them one below the other, about half an inch apart on the string, dropping as many links as you require to get them to hang evenly in the mouth, one below the other.

Mouthing Bits. I think those heavy old key mouthing bits are criminal things in a youngster's mouth, and heavy and bad for any other mouth, and utterly useless for re-making or refreshing.

A leading saddler used to make a chain with a spring hook at each end, and keys on the chain, which was good ; not so good as curb chains. Why not ? Oh, because it was expensive, and I hate spring hooks ; they are always getting caught up and in trouble.

Mouthing Two or Three-Year-Olds.
If you are going to give your two-year-olds and three-year-olds a bit of mouthing, let them first of all have one curb chain for about twenty minutes, when they are alone and loose in their box in the afternoon. After a few days you can, if you like, let them have it on whilst they are working, but I should not ; it only distracts their attention, and tends to get them into the habit of over bending. This, of course, refers to two-year-olds ; the three-year-olds can work in a light bridle, under their stable head collar (see long rein driving), and they can have a couple of hours in the afternoon, with two curb chains to amuse them.

Perhaps someone may read this who is quite a beginner, and say : " But how shall I know if I am succeeding and if I am improving and making the mouth ? " As long as your horse keeps working (playing and champing the chains), so surely are you doing good, but when they stop movement altogether, it is doing them no good. That is why, on a youngster, you must not leave the chains on too long at first, as the jaws might get a little tired, and the colt stop mouthing, and thereby get into the habit of never mouthing. **I never, on colt or aged horse, put the chain or chains absolutely the same height in the mouth every day ; as he may get used to them, and not play with them.**

Re-making Mouths. The re-making, or freshening of a mouth, is just the same process, only you must, as I stated previously, use three chains. Attach them in the same way to the stable head collar.

My horses, old and young, hunters, hacks, and all, instead of doing nothing in their stables in the afternoon, always had their chains on ; sometimes, if a horse would not start mouthing, I used to interlace a few long hairs, pulled out of a tail, into the links of one chain, and fasten the ends with a bit of cotton ; that generally had the desired effect, but was rarely necessary, because, on a very dry-mouthed horse, I used to let my bottom chains down to within an inch of his front teeth.

On a horse whose mouth I was re-making, I used to ring the changes between chains one day, and an old double bridle other days, the latter low in the horse's mouth, with the curb chain in his mouth instead of behind his jaw, his nose-band loose as possible, and the reins just attached to his roller by a bit of string.

This method I also used for three-year-olds, but the bridle had no reins; instead, I made reins of strong string, and I attached a curtain ring to the top of the roller, with another piece of string, untying the string reins from one side of his bridle, and passing them through the curtain ring, and then tying them the length I wanted them, to the other side of the bridle; never very short, but short enough to keep his head in the proper place; but the string reins running through the ring allowed him to turn his head as he wanted to.

I never fixed a horse by side reins, because my experience showed me that fixed school horses were like riding a board, whilst the other method produced the supple ride which is such a joy.

String over Check. You may come across a horse who hangs his head, and even if he works his mouthing chains, or bridle, does it in the vicinity of his knees.

Three rings, the bridoon (snaffle) of your double bridle and string, will stop this; let me explain how: One ring attached to the centre of the roller as before; the other two to act as bearing rein drops. You know how I mean, one each side of the horse's head; I like them just below the brow band, and to get them there, I take a piece of string about a foot or eighteen inches long, and pass one end through the loop of the brow band, over

MOUTHING

the top of the head, and down through the loop of the brow band the other side; then through one of the rings, and up again through the loop of the brow band, pulling the ring up to the loop; then pass the string over the head and down through the original loop of the brow band. You now have the two ends of your string side by side. Attach your remaining ring to them, pulling it up to the brow band, and you now have your drops ready.

Take a nice length of string and make your rein. There are two ways of doing this:

1. Tie one end of the string to brow band loop; thread string through bridoon ring, and up through drop ring; from there through ring on roller, back through drop ring on other side, down through bridoon ring, and bring it up and tie it to brow band loop, the length you want it.

It sounds complicated to a beginner, but take your book out to the stable, and put a bridle on a horse, and try; it is quite easy, and you will at once see the effect; and that you can place the head where you want it.

That is method No. 1, and is simply the old barouche horse bearing-rein—to be used in the stable or when leading, or long rein driving when mouthing and placing a horse, and my advice is: Do not use it tight or you will get your horse stiff and tired.

Now No. 2. Your rings are the same, but

c

this time you start by tying the end of your string to the bridoon; then up through the drop; down through the bridoon again; back through the ring on the roller, through the bridoon on the other side up through the drop, and down, and fasten it to the bridoon.

That one you can use in the stable, or long rein driving, or when mounted; only then, of course, you do away with the roller ring.

May I venture to point out to the jumping experts that this with the string short so as to just lie on the withers or neck, is a wonderful thing, if you want to bring one back on to his hocks quick in a cramped space.

One of the greatest hack experts I ever knew, used to show in a gag bridoon of this method; it took me quite a long time to fathom it.

Pillar Reins. Well, so much for mouthing, and just placing the head while mouthing. Although I am a great advocate of free mouthing for a horse in a loose box, I am also a great believer in the pillar reins; if you happen to have got a stall, expecially for youngsters, and by the way, brother beginner, do not ever put any mouthing tackle on a horse tied up in a stall without turning him round, and putting him on the pillar reins, or you will get him caught up on the manger or on something else.

What are pillar reins? Oh, a couple of

pieces of light cord attached to the stall posts, and then attached to each side of the head collar, tight enough for the horse not to be able to get them in his mouth and chew them. Lovely thing to have several horses in a long stable on the pillar reins, and watch them mouthing.

CHAPTER III

BITTING

A few reflections on bitting. We often hear the horse's mouth referred to, as the key to the situation. Well, what we want to find is the master-key, and I will give it to you in the single word:—Comfort.

Find the bit that suits your horse and that he goes comfortably in, and then there is comfort, for man and beast. But, having found the bit, do not imagine that you have a lasting key to the lock, you cannot ride a horse, at least, to get the best results, in the same bridle, year in, year out.

Well, first of all, never have your horse exercised in his own bridle. The best bit for exercise is a straight-barred snaffle; "Yes," a stallion bit, the finest change bridle for a groom there is. I am not talking to those of you who put an expert up, when you are not doing your own job, but to the man who sends his horse out to exercise.

Action of Plain Snaffle. Think for a moment, of the action of an ordinary plain snaffle, if you happen to have got it in the middle of the horse's mouth, it is a pinching action of the bars of the mouth or the lower jaw, caused by the joint in the bit. If you have not got it in the middle of his mouth, it is a pressure of the ring against one side, and a pinching action on the other side, from which it is difficult for the horse to escape. Not only that, but you will use this same bridle for leading, with the rein from the outside passed under the jaw, and then through the ring on the inside. Another rat-trap action.

Now think for a moment of a plain, straight bar, if you have got it in the middle of the horse's mouth, it is a level pressure. If you have *not* got it in the middle of the horse's mouth, it, like the jointed snaffle, has a pressure of the ring against the outside on the one side, but a level pressure on the other side, and the difference is, that, the moment a horse drops his head, the straight-barred snaffle falls into place in his mouth at once. For leading I need only say, that it must be the best bit, or the stallion men would not use it. I am not advocating the straight-barred snaffle as a riding bit, but as the bit which will do the least damage to your horse's mouth, when you are not riding him yourself.

The old-fashioned cheek snaffle was to my mind a better bit than the ring snaffle of the present day, but they went out of fashion a good many years ago. I have never used a "Puckle" snaffle, but I have heard them very well spoken of, and they look to me as if they might be an improvement on the ordinary ring snaffle. I should think that the best of all combinations would be a Puckle, with a straight bar, and when I start breaking horses again, that is one of the first bits that I shall experiment with, probably putting light mouthing keys in the middle of the bar.

My opinion of a snaffle is that it is only fit for racing, or for dealers to put on to hirelings, for bad horsemen to hold on to, and for grooms at exercise; and the golden exception that proves the rule, is, when you get a snaffled mouth horse. I once had one, you could ride him on one finger, in a snaffle; but how few people can ride a horse like that. I lent him to a friend who at once pulled him backwards into a ditch.

Double Bridle. I am not sure that a horse with too light a mouth, is not almost as difficult to deal with as a hard-mouthed horse. Probably the best all-round bridle is a medium cheeked double bridle, put nice and level in the horse's mouth that is to say that the bridoon does not wrinkle the corners of the mouth, and that the bit lies level just below it and the curb chain, so that when the bit comes back to its full extent it just touches the jaw, that was always my test bridle for a strange horse, and that was always the

BITTING

bridle that I aimed at getting my horses to go in.

You may find that it is not quite enough for your horse, then take one with the cheek a little longer and put it on the same way, better this than tightening the curb chain of your short cheek bridle, because the little bit of extra weight may do the trick and will cause no pain.

Banbury. Another good bit is a "Banbury," which you know is a double bridle with swinging cheek-pieces. Think of the action of this for a moment. What does it mean? That the two sides of the bit work separately, and it is the first bridle to try on a horse whose mouth is slightly uneven, by which I mean who is a little one-sided.

Pelhams. Then there are all sorts of "Pelhams" and I say at once and without hesitation, avoid the jointed Pelham, by which I mean the Pelham with a mouthpiece like a snaffle, for the obvious reason that it is a pure rat-trap action, pinching everywhere.

The best Pelham is a half-moon, many a horse with a light mouth will go perfectly on a half-moon Pelham, especially if you use a curb strap instead of a chain.

Rugby. Next to the half-moon Pelham comes the Rugby Pelham, it has a half-moon mouth-piece also, and a drop bridoon-ring. Why it is good, and why some horses love it I cannot tell you, I have never been able to fathom its action, but I can tell you that there are certain horses and a great many polo ponies on which it will prove the key for which you are looking.

Sefton. The Sefton, or egg-shaped Pelham, is a bit that I have found ponies go well in; it has an egg-shaped link in the middle of the mouth-piece, and the bars of the mouth-piece are half-moon.

Curb Chain on Pelham (Important). Now my reader, a golden rule as to how to put on the curb chain of a Pelham: bring it up through the bridoon ring and hook it outside. "Why is this a golden rule?" because with your curb chain put on like that it is impossible to pinch the corners of the mouth, and from being a very moderate bit, you turn your Pelham into one of the most useful bridles.

Please be quite sure that you understand how to put that curb chain on, it is one of the important things of this little book. I need hardly say that this does not apply to a Rugby Pelham, as it would spoil the action of the ring, so be very careful when using that bridle that you do not pinch the corners of the mouth. A very good way to avoid doing this is to use small, thick, leather cheek rings.

Before leaving the Pelham bit, I want to draw your attention to the bit used by nearly all the French cabmen, rather on the Pelham principle, but the great beauty of it is that the cheek-piece from the mouth-piece, to where the head-piece is stitched on, is so long, that when your curb is hooked on in the ordinary way there is no fear of pinching.

India-Rubber Bits. Now I think we have dealt with ordinary every-day bits; always buy a steel bit, never nickel, they break. India-rubber bits are dangerous and really unnecessary. The reason they are dangerous is that they have a small chain running through the india-rubber, and it rots and breaks at a critical moment.

Use of Inner Tube. The reason why I say they are unnecessary, is because, if you cut up an old inner tube of a motor tyre and wrap it round the mouth-piece, either singly or doubly, tying it round with a piece of string, you have got something very nearly as good, and while we are talking of inner tubes, a bit of inner tube round your curb chain, very frequently, turns what you think a hard-mouthed and pulling horse into a nice easy-mouthed horse. "Why does it do it?" because he finds something soft that does not hurt him behind the jaw, and he does not twist and pull to get away from it.

Another good curb guard is to pass your curb chain through a little piece of hose-pipe.

Hanoverian or Running Rein. I have not made any mention of "Hanoverian" bits, Pelham or otherwise, they are very sharp and are bits that should only be used by an expert. I think if you have got a horse that pulls so much that you think he requires a Hanoverian, you will do better to try him with a running rein, on the same principle as I explained for the one-sided mouthed horse, only used on both sides. It is far less punishing, and can be brought into action as much or as little as required.

Lip Strap. Do not use a double bridle or Pelham without a lip strap, it is wrong, this little strap has two uses, one : If the horse throws his head, it prevents the bit from coming up and over. Two : it prevents a horse from catching hold of the cheek of his bit.

Gags. I am not a great advocate of the use of gags, except by good horsemen. They are very useful if you have a horse who rakes at his bridle in his gallop, used instead of a bridoon with double bridle or with an ordinary snaffle. You will find two or three different types of gags sold by the big saddlers, I think the snaffle gag, i.e., a snaffle with a slip rein running through holes in its rings, is the best and the least punishing. I see they are much in vogue amongst the polo fraternity, used with a single rein, a good bit in the hands of a good horseman, but a cruel bit in the hands of a rough horseman.

The One-Sided Mouth. Now I want to consider for a moment the one-sided mouth,

BITTING 43

that we referred to in Mouthing. When you have got a difficulty or something wrong, I always think the best thing to do is to try and trace its origin. I have already affirmed that I believe no such thing as a one-sided mouthed horse was ever foaled, therefore one-sidedness must come from the way he was broken in, because he cannot very well contract a one-sided mouth while he is running about as a youngster. That is why I am perfectly sure that all long rein driving should be done on a stable head collar (see Long Rein Driving), or it may come from the man who breaks him using one side of the mouth more than the other.

I have noticed that it is generally the near side of the mouth which is hard, this probably may be attributed to the English rule of the road. I think the hands of very few people are absolutely level, but this would only account for the horses who are just slightly one-sided. The horse who is absolutely dead one side of his mouth, I attribute to bad breaking.

The best way to deal with the one-sided mouthed horse is as I have already said, try a Banbury bit, if it does not work try a Pelham, with a piece of inner tube rolled round the mouth-piece on the side which he does not respond to, make it a good thick wad of indiarubber, tie it with string, and do not forget to tie the ends of your string round the cheek-piece of your bridle to prevent the inner tube slipping across to the other side. I have found that one of the best cures.

There is the old fashioned way of putting a leather cheek-piece with little points like drawing pins to run into his cheek, but it is a nasty barbaric method, and even though he may respond owing to the pain you will not cure him by it, you will only prevent him doing it for the time being, there will be no improvement when you take your cheek leather off.

If you have got a confirmed bad-sided horse, and you want to use a prevention, my advice is : a running rein attached to the girth tabs under the flap of your saddle, through the bit, and back to your hand; but, as I say, it is a prevention not a cure.

Tongue Over Bit. Another thing we have got to deal with is a horse who gets his tongue over the bit; bad breaking again is responsible for this. I know that when he was being broken he got into the habit of it, or he has rolled his tongue back to try and alleviate the pain that the bit is causing him.

It is a difficult thing to cure, the only cure for it that I know is to take a broad tape and tie it round the tongue as high up as possible, leaving the two ends of about six inches each, and tie these firmly under the jaw. With this tape on he cannot get his tongue over the bit, and once he gets out of the habit he very often gives it up altogether.

A lot of bad mouths and hard mouths are due to the tongue being over the bit, and many people never think to look. The first time you take your horse out without the tape, take your bit up higher than usual in his mouth and keep it there for a day or two, but be very careful to watch that he does not get back to the habit of putting his tongue over again.

You can buy all sorts of bits with grids and ports on them to prevent a horse getting his tongue over, but I often found that that led to a horse rolling his tongue behind the bit.

Buying Bits. The way I used to buy my bits was by going to "Tattersalls'"; you very often find bridles done up in bundles, you very rarely want them all but there may be one or two useful ones, and I used to make a bundle of what I did not want and put them in the next week's sale. In this way I added to my collection of bits quite cheaply.

Before leaving the bitting question, I want to add that I never went out hacking or nagging without at least one spare curb chain and a bit of string in my pocket, and if a horse was not going comfortably in his bridle, I used to put the spare curb chain in his mouth and make him mouth and play with his bit.

I shall deal with the fitting of a bridle in

another chapter, but let me say here, that although I am perfectly aware that strapping a nose band up tight prevents a horse from keeping his mouth open, that again, is a prevention, not a cure. The cure must come from the bit, he is surely holding his mouth open hoping to avoid pain.

You may have a fancy, especially if you are showing a riding horse or hack, to use a single rein bridle, for this you have only got to take the snaffle off a double bridle : and every now and again it is a very good change for a horse, and he will go very well in it, but I have never seen a horse yet that you could ride constantly in a single rein bit, and I need hardly say that it should only be used on a finished horse, and never on any horse that is not bridle-wise.

CHAPTER IV

BREAKING AND TRAINING, UP TO THREE YEARS OLD

Never use any article of saddlery, strap, string, cord, web, or girth that might break.

The above, I think, is perhaps the first thing to remember when you are starting upon the education of a young horse. It is not a bad thing to remember at all times, that a broken leather or girth may not only give you a nasty fall, but may spoil a good day's fun or season's polo.

Begin with Brood Mare. And now we will start on the training of a foal, and I hope I shall not upset my readers by saying, that his education should start before he is born, by which I mean, getting your brood mares quiet and handy while in foal, so that you can walk up to them always when at grass.

The easiest way to achieve this is a tit-bit of corn, carrot, bread, or anything when you visit them in the field or stable. This way you will save the mare trying to get away when she has her foal at foot, and not only save knocking his baby legs about by following her, but, and just as important, establish in his wee brain an idea of friendliness from the outset, when he sees his Mother come to meet you instead of cantering away.

Handling Foal. If you start a foal in the way it should go, you will probably save many a battle in after-life.

Teach your foal to lead, employing only a head collar, and handle it well all over by rubbing and stroking all over its body and limbs. I need not add head and neck because as an animal lover, that will be your first action.

Remember the little chap is timid, and it is up to you at this stage to establish confidence between him and mankind for life, unless he falls into the hands of some brute who breaks his confidence by ill-treating him.

How to teach a Foal to Lead. When he is good and strong on his legs, running out with his Mother, about eight weeks old, take up your mare into a box or yard, the former for choice, then get someone to go in with you to hold the mare's head, and lead her round as you want her and quiet her, because she will fret when you catch her foal.

Get the foal into a corner and gently soothe it, till you get a chance to slip a hemp halter or something soft round his neck, then put the head collar on and handle it a little. That is enough for the moment, go back

Breaking and Training

presently and get hold of the head collar, your aid having hold of the mare, attach your lead, and have the mare led round the yard or box, following quite close, or right up alongside with the foal. Remember you are establishing confidence.

Then gradually get out into a field, still following, so little by little, in a day or so turn away from the mare, until you arrive at being able to go anywhere alone ; that ends your foal's education, but keep him in constant practise, even if it is only for ten minutes once a week, but much better than that is a few yards when you feed, when they come to meet you.

Either whilst with their Mother, or after separation, lead one or other to the place you feed them. My advice is : always to leave a head collar on your foal for this purpose, but be sure and see that there is plenty of room in it. How often one sees horses out at grass chafed, because the head collar touches when they eat.

Teach Foals to Back. Let me add here, teach your foal to back, and every time you touch him back him a step or two. The same applies to every youngster you are training, and every horse you are re-training, each time you go into the box back him one or two steps.

Yearlings. The education of a yearling (and I think I ought to say here, as I have said in my Foreword, I am not referring to race-horses, as I know nothing about them) is much the same as that of a foal, just carry on, keeping him accustomed to being handled and led.

If you have got to start on a yearling who has never been handled or touched, get him in a box and get the head collar on him, with a long web rein attached to it. Handle him, and get him to lead round the box, then get him outside and lead him about.

Some people let their yearlings have a run round on a long rein, it is a matter of opinion, I think it depends very much upon whether you have a good place to do it or not. You must have good going, not too hard and not too deep, because, remember a youngster's bone is very soft and you may easily cause a permanent injury.

Two-Year-Olds. Your two-year-old, if it has never been handled before, you will first of all deal with in the same way as your yearling, and then put him on the long reins for a little as described in Long Rein Driving. Of course only using a stable head collar, and you ought to be able to use your felt pad under the nose band all the time on a two-year-old, so as to avoid making his nose sore.

Putting Roller on Colt. Before you turn him out again, accustom him to a roller,

Breaking and Training 51

that is to say, one day when you have got him going nicely on the long reins and he is nice and warm, pop a roller on to him, do not flop it down on to the middle of his back, put it on his withers and slide it gently into position. Always have a breaststrap on this roller to prevent his bucking through it, do up your breaststrap first, now do up your roller, do not pull it tight but just so that it touches him all round. He is sure to blow himself out, so after the first buck is over you will probably be able to take it up two or more holes.

If you have got somebody with you, let him hold him, and get out to the end of your long reins, paying a good deal of attention to your inner rein.

Now let your assistant stand clear and set your colt in motion (see Long Rein Driving), he is sure to plunge and buck, but having already got him broken to the long reins and having chosen a good open space, he cannot hurt himself, so let him have his buck out. Take him back to his stable or yard, or wherever you keep him, and keep his roller on him for four or five hours. If you repeat this method for a few days you will be able to put the roller on him in the same way as on an old horse.

For the Mouthing of Two or Three-Year-Olds (see Mouthing). The education of a three-year-old, if you have had him as a yearling or two-year-old, is merely the same as a two-year-old, unless you decide to back him, in which case see chapter on Backing and Training. The three-year-old requires more mouthing (see Mouthing), and should be completely broken to the long reins (see Long Rein Driving).

CHAPTER V

BACKING AND RIDING A COLT, AND RE-TRAINING OF OTHER HORSES

Education of Four-year-olds. If you have had the handling, as described in the previous chapter, of your four-year-old, he will be ready to back as soon as you get him up, after he has had two or three days refreshing his memory on what he learnt as a three-year-old.

If you have not had the education of this four-year-old, but have bought him, either as a grass colt, just handled enough to have been led and put in a horse box, or from Ireland, where, after the fashion of the majority of young horses, he may have been broken with a snaffle bridle and a big stick, or in the plough, then my advice is, start him with your long reins and bring him up-to-date with them before you attempt riding him.

Re-training of other Horses. The same applies to any other horse that you may buy and wish to bring to your way of riding. With these latter you will, of course, not have to go into the details when you come to ride them, which I am going into now, as regards saddling, etc., but to get them supple and handy, the long reins are essential.

Saddling. We will now take it that your four-year-old has completed his education on the long reins, and you decide to saddle him. Put your saddle on in precisely the same way that you did the roller, that is to say, place it on his withers and slide into position, gently tightening your girths. Take a piece of string or a spare stirrup leather and pass it from stirrup to stirrup loosely underneath him, to prevent your stirrups flopping about.

Then give him a good twisting and turning on the long reins with his saddle on. The day you are going to back him let him have a good dose of long reins and have him a bit weary.

Backing a Colt. There are two methods of backing a horse: the one if you are a very fine young horseman and love a good shake up—then let somebody hold him, take the string or stirrup leather off that is securing your stirrups, do away with one half of your long reins, thus turning your other half into a long web lead. Put a straight-barred snaffle, with a good strong single rein on. Let your assistant give you a leg-up and hold the colt until you are comfortable, then let him lead him on and lead him about, twisting and turning for a minute or two, until you decide

Backing and Riding a Colt

to put him on the circle, and if he is a cheery one to let him have his buck out. My advice to you, fine horseman though you be, is to put on that best of all friends, the martingale neck strap to hold on to. Your job is to sit there, do not worry about your reins, your assistant has got him on a long rein, you hang on, never let him put you down, or he may never forget, and throughout his life, from time to time, experiment, and often succeed with a less good horseman, which will not enhance your reputation as a horse breaker.

That is one method of backing a young horse, the other method is : when you have finished with him on the long reins, after you have put his saddle on, take him into his loose box or a small yard, let your assistant, who has his web lead as before, give you a lift so that you lie on your chest across the saddle, pat your colt and talk to him, now let him be led up a stride, now two or three strides, now get off, now on again, lead him a little more, back him a stride or two, now gently raise yourself into the saddle and let him be led about the box. Get on and off three or four times, do this for a day or two, when you bring him from his work, and then when you find he is happy and confident after you have done it, one morning get him out in the field and ride him about a bit with your assistant leading him. He is sure to have his buck out, but it will not be such a hearty one as with the previous method, because he will be bucking to see if he can get rid of you, but without surprise and fear, which the colt who was suddenly mounted probably felt.

Now you have got him quietly riding about, begin to steer him with the reins. I quote the old cavalry drill book once more : " The inner rein leading, a pressure of the outer rein on his neck supporting."

Early Training. You are beginning from the very commencement, to make your horse " bridlewise," as the Americans call it, which I consider a most comprehensive term.

Start your turns and circles at a walk, you will ride him about quietly for a few days in the snaffle, letting him get thoroughly accustomed to you, and for those few days, my advice is : a little trotting, and a little cantering, and then backing, but on the straight, and through all this early training, very short spells of anything, with two or three minutes rest between each spell, because the muscles of his back are unaccustomed to carrying weight ; the circulation stops, he feels like you feel when you put a puttee on too tight, or have something pressing on a muscle. You will quickly sicken him if the periods are prolonged, whereas for a few minutes he will give you his full attention.

You need not waste the rest intervals, far from it, you will begin his education from the ground, a flexing of the muscles of the

BACKING AND RIDING A COLT

neck, and the movement of his forehand and hindquarters separately. And now we will deal with those points, so easy, so useful, so often forgotten, or not known, and yet perhaps the largest part of the key to the secret of a perfectly broken horse.

As I have said elsewhere, to be a perfect ride, every muscle must be well flexed and supple, a horse that you have got to pull round, however nice and easy he may be in his paces, can never be a perfect ride, and to get that perfect ride he must turn at the least touch of the neck, or the lightest pressure of a leg or heel. To get him to turn to the touch of a rein the muscles of the neck must have been well flexed, so as I said we will occupy our rest intervals, when he has had a moment or two's complete repose and you have lighted your pipe or cigarette (and here a word of advice, never ride your youngster or an awkward horse with a pipe in your mouth. I have seen a horse throw up his head and drive the mouthpiece of a pipe into the roof of a man's mouth). I hope you smoke, as the mere action of lighting a pipe or cigarette, after you have been very concentrated upon riding your young horse, is repose, and if you have been feeling a wee bit " edgy " because, perhaps, he has not been going quite as you think he might have been, you will start off quite fresh again.

May I say here, that if you are inclined to

be a bit short-tempered, and you find yourself going to pick up your stick or convey your mood through your hands to your horse, pull up quick before you do any damage, and get off and give him a pat, think about something else, and start afresh in a few minutes. To bring oneself to do this is worth anything, and this, my readers, is by one who knows, because I am red-headed and short of temper, and I trained myself first of all to do as I have prescribed and from that to have the utmost patience with a horse.

Flexing Neck Muscles. And now this muscle-flexing business; stand beside your horse and take up a rein in each hand if you have got a snaffle on, if you have got a double bridle, take up a snaffle rein in each hand, now gently feel and play with the outer rein. I want you to get your horse to turn his head away from you without moving his feet, steady him with the inner rein, and play that outer rein. The minute he does it ever so little, stop and pat him, repeat it two or three times till he gets the idea; now go round the other side and do the same thing, gradually getting him to bring his head further and further round, till he almost touches his shoulder.

Afterwards do the same thing mounted. By doing this you have flexed that muscle behind his ears and jaw, and it is my opinion that this muscle affects the whole of the

Backing and Riding a Colt

spine. It will only take you two or three lessons to achieve this, some horses come to it at once.

In the case of re-making horses when they are strong and you have not to give continual rests, I used to go into a box and pop a bridle on and do all this ground-work whenever I had a spare half-hour.

Movement of Fore Feet. Now to teach him to be bridlewise and obedient to the leg. We will start on the ground. Take hold of the reins with one hand, behind the jaws close up to the bit, now try to make him move his off front foot over to the right, the minute he does it without moving his back feet, stop and pat him; now his near foot a little to the left, increase this so that one foot follows the other, and keep him on till, shuffling his hind feet round, his front feet have described a complete circle.

This will come in a few days. At the same period as you are teaching him this you can be teaching him to do the same thing with his hind feet.

Movement of Hind Feet. Cut yourself a couple of long thin sticks about as thick as your first finger and about five or six feet long, take hold of your horse as for moving his forehand, and take one of your sticks and tap him lightly *along his side*, keeping his forehand steady with the hand holding his bridle as before. Pat him the minute he moves his hind feet, to show him that he has done what you want him to do; keep on gradually until he can describe a full circle either way with his hind feet. Now you have prepared him to learn the use of the rein against the neck, and the use of the leg.

How to Hold Reins When Schooling. Then get on him, and after you have had a jog round and got his head nicely placed, pull him up. Let me say here that I think the best way of holding your reins for all school work is two reins in each hand, the curb rein under your little finger, up through the palm of your hand and out between the first and second fingers, the snaffle rein over your first knuckle, the end falling down through the palm of the hand. Thus, to raise his head, you draw your snaffle backwards and forwards through his mouth, and to lower his head or bend his neck, you turn your little fingers towards you. This method was taught me by a French high-school master, and I have found it the most useful way of putting a horse's head into position.

Bridlewise. The next stage is the circling education. You have brought your horse to a standstill, back him a couple of steps to get his balance right, and now try moving his forehand with his hindquarters quite steady. Have one of your long sticks in each hand

Backing and Riding a Colt

to steady his quarters if necessary. If you want him to move to the right, lead with your right rein, pressing the left lightly against his neck, keep him up with your legs so that he does not run back, and the minute he moves his front as you want him to do, stop and show him that he has done right. You may find it necessary to keep one of those long sticks along his side to prevent him moving his hind-quarters; as soon as he has got the idea do away with that pressure of the long stick and gradually lessen the leading of that inner rein, so that he comes to move at the least touch of the outer rein against his neck, and that is how you teach a horse to be "bridlewise."

Answer to Leg. To teach him to answer to the leg. You have taught him on the ground to answer to that long stick by laying it right along his side, now you want him to circle his hind-quarters using his forehand as a pivot; touch him with an elastic pressure of the outer leg, tapping him with the long stick right along his side. I emphasise these words, *right along his side*, because I do not want you to bring your stick straight down behind your leg, as you want to keep that part as fresh as possible for the leg.

Now keep his hind-quarters moving both ways, first one and then the other, with stick and leg, and as the lessons proceed gradually dispense with the stick.

The day that you can do away with the stick altogether, and make him describe a complete figure of eight, one loop with his fore feet circling round his hind feet, and the other with his hind feet round his fore feet, you can consider you are well on the way to having a really broken horse, at any rate you have got a horse that answers to leg and rein.

The Passage. To get him to " passage," which you have already taught him on the long reins, you will do with a combination of leg and reins. At first let his forehand lead a good deal, as it is easier for him, but afterwards you will get him to quite square.

Reining Back. I do not think I have made enough comment in this chapter on the use of reining back. Make your horse take a step or two back every minute or two, never let him have his head down while he is backing, or while he is doing any of his work; it is an easy thing to get a horse's head down, but it is terribly difficult to get it up. So you must keep playing that bit backwards and forwards through his mouth to keep his head up, backing two or three strides with his head up, and then a steady halt, and moving forward, still collected.

Standing Still whilst Mounting. Another point I wish to emphasise is teaching your horse to stand still while you are mounting or dismounting. Nothing is more annoying

Backing and Riding a Colt

than a horse which starts to go on, or walk round in a circle when you put your foot in the stirrup to mount, or moves just as you are getting off.

If you make a point of this from the very beginning you will have no difficulty; but if you find a horse that you are re-training will not stand still, the best way to teach him is by getting him against a wall, and taking your reins short, inner reins the shortest, putting your foot in the stirrup and raising yourself up and down until you can do it without his moving. Then take him a little further away from the wall and repeatedly get on and off him.

When you have got your horse bridlewise, and to answer to the leg, teach him all his turns and circles at the walk, then at a slow and very collected jog. Make sure that he learns to make his turns square, not that he falls away with a lurch the minute you touch him with rein or leg.

Of course if you have got a school, this is easy enough, but if you have not, mark yourself out a suitable piece of ground with corner stones, and when you are riding about training in a field always ride on a mark, so as to be sure your horse is going straight, otherwise you will find that he is developing a habit of edging away to one side or other, probably to the side where the gate and his stables may lie.

When you have been doing a bit of fast work with him, drop back into the slowest of hack canters before you pull up. A perfectly broken horse should be able to be fully extended, and then brought back to a dead slow canter, and the reins dropped on his neck. I think perhaps this takes more teaching than most things, and can only be done by the use of the voice.

Punishment. I have not mentioned anything about punishing a horse, or the use of a stick, very few men know how to hit a horse, and I only say this : if you are going to hit him, hit him quick, straight down the shoulder and put your stick away while he is still wondering where it came from. Do not be led away with the temptation to keep on hitting him. Remember what you are hitting him for and get it over.

I say this because sometimes the mere action of hitting a horse seems to make one want to go on, and it is not until afterwards that you discover what a fool, and how unkind, you have been. Never hit a horse about the head—this is a golden rule (and like all golden rules, has an exception)—except when he is standing straight up on end with you, then if you are master enough of the art, you can pick up your stick and hit him smartly between the ears, but take care you do not lose your balance, or you will pull him over backwards, and frankly, unless it is very well

Backing and Riding a Colt

done, I do not think you are going to do the least good.

Changing Stick Over. Remember if you are going to use your stick, you must cultivate the art of changing it from hand to hand, and of hitting your horse on either side. How often do you see some moderate horseman, whose horse has refused a little fence with him, swerving to the left, put him at the fence again, pick up his stick and hit him down his right shoulder, thus driving him to the left once more. The reason why he has done it, is because he does not know how to hit him on his near side; but believe me, brother beginner, the more you keep your hands down and use your legs, and the less you use that stick, the better.

The One-way Horse. You may come across a horse that you are re-training, who will only turn one way: the long reins period is the time to break him of this habit, and as you gradually get him to turn the way you want him to do, and you get on his back, be sure you try that turn a few times at the walk first with everything in his favour, by that I mean—towards his home, and for a few days never ask him to turn away from home, until you have got him so much in the habit that he has practically forgotten all about the bad habit.

If you happen to have a little wood anywhere handy near your place, you can take him in there and jog him round by different paths, that is a splendid way to muddle a horse. And so, my reader, I will leave you to get on with your training, and ask you to remember that very often when you think he is not trying, it is only that he does not exactly understand what you require.

Inspecting Saddlery. Let me add: never forget to look round your horse before you get on; see that his saddlery is right in every detail. Never put your foot into the stirrup till you have run your fingers down inside his girth; it will become a habit and an invaluable one.

On the 4th of June, 1916, I was out in Salonika with a mounted brigade, we were right up country, but as luck would have it, our mail had come in that day, and our parcels from "Fortnum and Mason" had produced, as well as some good things to eat, several bottles of champagne and whiskey, and there gathered together under a tree that night some six or eight Old Etonians to celebrate the 4th of June. We were having a merry time, when in rode one of our Greek intelligence men on his rough native pony. We invited him to join us, and drink flowed freely, he was not used to mixing whiskey and champagne, and if I remember right, some of Fortnum and Mason's cocktail mixture, and soon began to get very chatty.

Backing and Riding a Colt

I suppose that talking over old school-days had made me feel young again, and by way of a joke I got up and went over to where his pony was standing behind some bushes, and crossed his reins, and fixed his girths so that his saddle would come round when he put his foot in the stirrup. Some time later, very much under the influence of drink, he rolled towards his pony, and drunk though he was, and you can take it from me he was drunk, the first thing he did, was to look at his bridle, and then at his girths. Now that was pure habit of this natural horseman, he could not have had the faintest idea that I had been out to his pony, and so it must have been force of habit.

How many people do you see whose horse is brought to the door, or get out of their car at the meet to get on to their hunter, or go across to get on their pony for a chukkah of polo, who look over their saddlery before they get on ? Try to acquire this good habit.

CHAPTER VI

STABLE MANAGEMENT

The Master's Eye. I am not going deeply into stable management and feeding, there are many good books which deal at length with these questions, and, as I have already said in my Foreword, so much depends on the length of one's purse and local conditions. Our old friend "Mr. Jorrocks," however, gives us a very good motto, "A master's eye is worth two pairs of 'ands"; and I do not care how good a stud groom or person you may have in charge of your horse or horses, personal supervision is absolutely necessary, both for economy and for keeping things up to the mark. Not necessarily because you distrust your man, but it is very much nicer for him, and he will take much more interest in his work if he feels you are going to take a thorough interest in every minor detail.

I do not mean go about meddling, changing a horse's feed, and giving orders to underlings which is some people's idea of supervision; that only upsets your head man. No two people can feed one horse, and no man can serve two masters, but if you are not satisfied with the looks of a certain horse you can suggest a change of feeding; or again, if you find a horse dirty, do not go to the groom who is grooming him, but go and bite your head groom and let him pass it on.

Hygiene. Let us run through a few points which are the stud groom's job to overlook, and yours to glance at casually, and see that they are done. First of all absolute cleanliness is necessary; however good the drainage system of your stables, be sure that disinfectant is poured down the drains at least twice a week, say on Wednesday and Saturday mornings.

Be sure the mangers are kept perfectly clean; you do not like eating off a dirty plate or drinking out of a dirty cup, and a horse's sense of smell is, I forget how many times, more acute than yours; but I should think, that sour bran, to him must smell like a decaying corpse.

Make certain that the walls of your stable, especially round the manger, are kept perfectly clean; also that the floor is kept clean, a rather difficult thing, even when you have a good cement floor with drainage grooves, but I do not advocate the washing of the floor of a box or stable that is in use, more than you can help, especially in winter, because it is difficult to get it perfectly dry before the bedding is replaced.

Strawing. You will find it difficult to get the present day stable man to muck out a box properly, he will either throw out perfectly good straw or he will leave a lot of wet bedding underneath the fresh straw he is putting in ; this to save himself the trouble of carting it away. Pay regular visits to your manure heap to correct the first fault, and turn up your horse's bedding to correct the second.

Moss Litter. You may not be able to get straw ; you may live in a part of the world where the price is prohibitive, so you may have to use peat moss litter. Be sure if you do, that before it is put down, a good wisp of hay or straw is rammed down your drain ; and afterwards, that all wet moss litter is carefully removed several times a day.

Watch your horse's feet and do not forget that moss litter is very dusty stuff, so that your man must be most particular as regards the sponging out of the horse's eyes and nostrils.

Architecture of Stabling. If you are building a stable, have overhead ventilation and high bottom doors, so that a horse can just look over ; that is to say, one-third top door and two-thirds bottom door, then you can leave him loose with his top door open, and he can look out and breathe the fresh air without the least danger of his trying to jump out.

Ventilation. Overhead ventilation is most necessary, and if you come by a stable that is already built and has that most iniquitous thing, men's rooms over the horses, then get ventilators put in as near to the ceiling as possible, as all the bad gases rise to the top. More horses catch cold through being too hot than too cold; an extra blanket and a cold stable is a great secret of health.

Clothing. See that the clothing is comfortably put on him, and that the breast straps of the rugs, or the breast strap of the roller are not too tight; that the roller is just tight enough to prevent the rugs from slipping.

One word here to our brother beginner. When you take a friend into your stable to show him your horse, undo the breast straps and unbuckle the roller, then sweep the clothing off over his tail, this will leave his coat laying flat and he will look as if he has just been wiped over with a rubber; also the person who is with you, if knowledgeable, will say: " This fellow knows."

Head Collars. Be sure that there is plenty of room in the stable head collar for the jaw to work. I was horrified one day in going into a stable where there was a stud of lovely horses to see that all the head collars were too small. I mentioned it to my host, who turned round to his stud groom, and said:

"Why didn't you tell me that these head collars were not big enough ?" Now this was a case of pure lack of personal supervision, because my host was a man who knew.

Rack Chains. Great care should be taken that the spring hooks of the rack chains are always in good order. I saw a horse's nostril torn right out on a broken rack chain hook; again lack of personal supervision, and I was the person.

Cleaning. Keep an eye to the cleaning of the head collar and roller, if you use a leather roller, and I should; they are expensive, but they wear much longer than web ones. I say, an eye to the cleaning of rollers and head collars, because they do not go into the cleaning room, and sometimes it is too much trouble to go and fetch the soap, sponge, and polishing rag, down to the loose box.

Water. Always keep water with your horse. I said I was not going to lay down any hard and fast rules; I will not; but I will say this: "I beg of you, whoever you are, always keep water with your horse." Do not be influenced by people who say it is wrong; do not be influenced by people who talk of colic; I had two cases of colic in fifteen years, both the same mare, she was subject to it; but keep water always with your horse. Nature, I understand, enables the camel to carry a supply of water to last him over a certain period, but it did not furnish the horse with a like reservoir. The poor horse who is only watered at regular intervals, which, I regret to say, are sometimes very irregular intervals, drinks as much as he can hold in self-defence, but the horse who has got water with him and knows that he is going to have water with him, drinks as nature dictates. You go quietly down to your stable yard after midday feed, when the men have gone to dinner, or in the evening when the horses have been done up; you will see them eat a little, then drink a little, and keep quietly on between manger or hay, and water. Surely that will prove I am right. If water is not kept constantly in the stable, then be sure to water your horse *before* you feed him.

Watering Hunters and Tired Horses.
Moderation in all things, and what I have laid down about water, should naturally be moderated if you bring in a very beat hunter, when you will give him gruel (if it has not been possible to give him some on the way home), or chilled water; then, when he is done over, you will give him a little more chilled water, and when you have seen him or heard him eat a bit, you will fill up his water manger or bucket with chilled water; but as you are strong, be merciful, and before you go to bed, go and see that the bucket or water manger is filled up. Do you not know yourself if you have had an awfully gruelling day, when you wake up in the night, or at dawn, you are

very often thirsty. I am sure it is the same with a horse.

I know there are many people who will not agree with me, but I do not believe that a few swallows of water hurt a horse at any time, even if he is sweating when out hunting. You come to water; let him just take two or three swallows, not drink his fill. "But," you say to me, "where does your nature come in, why should he want to drink his fill?" My answer is: "Nature has not told him that he has to go on chasing the fox, and that you are not turning to hack gently home, because if you were, you would let him drink his fill."

At the beginning of the war, I had a Squadron of reserve Cavalry regiment. I used to drum this water theory into the heads of my subalterns and non-commissioned officers and men till they were sick of it. One day in Salonika I met a fellow who had been in my squadron, and I said to him: "Your horse is looking well," he said, "Yes, sir, and entirely thanks to you teaching me about water." I first learnt this most important point of horsemastership from (as he was then) Squadron Sergeant Major Olden, who was Squadron Sergeant Major of the famous C Squad, of my regiment, during the South African war. He was a born horsemaster and told me many things, but above all, he told me that throughout the South African

Stable Management 75

war, whenever he could water his horses he did so, and whatever I have been doing with horses since then I have followed his example, and proved his words times without number

Feeding. As I said before, I am not going very minutely into the question of feeding; it depends upon so many things; two horses may do exactly the same work; one may require the most delicate feeding, whereas, on a couple of feeds a day, and a bit of hay, the other horse carries perfect condition.

I said also that two men cannot feed one horse; I was, of course, referring to hunters and polo ponies, and horses that are doing fast work and have to be kept in good condition for long periods. The way you can help your head man most, is by giving him a rough idea, if possible, of what work you are proposing to do with your horses during the coming week, or in the immediate future. Also you can help him by telling him if you notice anything out of the ordinary that your horse passes during the time he is out.

By the way, here is a very useful hint from a well-known stud owner and breeder, which can be heartily endorsed: After weaning the foals, feed them for two or three weeks with soft food, and let them nibble a little hay or green stuff; then, in order to get rid of any worms, mix a worm powder in the food, and repeat after another couple of weeks or so if you find it necessary.

Forage. With regard to the buying of your forage, be careful to buy good clean stuff; the big fat milky oat is not always the best feed; a good medium clean oat, with a nice tender husk is just as good as the oat that you can squeeze a good fat kernel out of and retain a coarse husk in your hand.

I do not believe in laying down so much corn per horse, per day; if your man is a clever feeder and you have given him a rough idea of what work the horse is going to do, he can feed accordingly. Some horses require more corn than others, and when you are teaching a horse, you are never going to get the best result if he is mad fresh, and full of corn.

Hay should be clean and sweet smelling; if you are buying it in bales, be sure and open one or two and see that they are all right in the centre.

Bran should, if possible, be nice big flakes; take some in the palm of your hand and rub it with the fingers of your other hand, the softer and more mealy it feels the better the feed.

Epsom Salts. A little Epsom salts in the bran mash on the Saturday night is a fine thing for purifying the blood. Put about a dessert-spoonful, per horse, into a bottle and

Stable Management

fill it three parts full with very hot water, shake it up till the salts are thoroughly dissolved ; now pour this into the bucket of water that the mash is going to be mixed with, and stir the water, then you will be quite sure that the salts will be well distributed in the mash. My advice to you is : take trouble to see that the mash is nice and dry, and thoroughly mixed. Mix it first of all with a broom handle or stick, cover it with a sack and let it stand for a couple of hours, now mix it again with your hands until you feel it has become of a nice drying substance.

Use of Tobacco. A little piece of plug tobacco is a very fine thing for a horse or dog, they say that no worms will ever stay inside an animal with a bit of tobacco. A horse gets to love it, and I used to give it to my horses in the same way as you give a bit of sugar. I learnt this from an old man who came into my stable off the road one day ; I took him on, and he was the sort of stableman who could do his four horses and have his corner of the yard looking like a new pin, while some of the other men were grooming one horse. I saw him give a horse something one day ; I said, " What's that ? " He was a man of few words, he said " Plug." His horses looked better and carried more shine than any of the others, and I found that it was not only because he was an expert groom, but the tobacco had a lot to do with it.

Sugar. I hate the habit of going into a horse's box and giving him a bit of sugar, it leaves a sweet taste in his mouth, and he goes and licks his manger, and you go in a few days afterwards and you find him laying hold of it; and that was how he learnt crib biting. At the same time sugar is a very fine stimulant, and if you use it on a weak horse that is in very poor condition, you may obtain excellent results. Also on a horse that is very exhausted, a little sugar in the gruel is a fine thing, but be sure if you are giving it to a horse as a stimulant, that you keep his manger well sponged inside and out.

Green Food. I am a great believer in green food and carrots, and at the time of year when you can get these, you can dispense with the use of salts. In the days when we used to have warmer weather in England, I sent my horses out grazing a good deal.

Rock Salt. A lump of rock salt is a good thing in the manger, but real brown rock salt; not the stuff that is prepared in a sort of brick to hang up on the wall.

Horse's Feet. Pay great attention to your horse's feet; see that they are kept properly picked out and that the coronets are kept well greased. The coronet is a sort of indiarubber substance, and cracked hoofs generally come from the coronet being too dry.

Stable Management

Eyelashes. It is a habit of many grooms, for smartness sake, to singe or cut a horse's eyelashes. They were given to him as feelers in the dark; it is cruel to rob him of them.

Twitch. Eliminate from your stable that iniquitous thing, a twitch. A twitch, brother beginner, is an old bit of broom handle with a loop of string passed through it, and it is used by pulling the horse's upper lip through the loop and twisting the handle till the string is tight, thus causing him a great deal of pain. This instrument is generally put on whilst a tail is being pulled (never put a pair of scissors on a tail except to square off the end), or a ticklish horse is being groomed or clipped, or sometimes at the forge whilst a horse is being shod.

I will give you a much better contrivance: take a piece of thin cord, make a loop in one end of it, and pass the cord over the horse's head, see that the loop hangs about level with his cheekbone, bring the cord up under his upper lip, and pass it through the loop, now pull this up as tight as you want it. You can tie it if necessary, if you are alone, but a better way is, if somebody is holding the horse, for him to hold the end of the cord in his hand, and if the horse attempts to kick or is troublesome, to tighten it or give it a light jerk. This bit of string is a most valuable asset, and was taught me by Major Dibble, riding master of the Cavalry School,

Netheravon. You can use it with a bridle on if you want to, and it is a first-class way of curing a horse that kicks at you as you are mounting, a habit that he has probably acquired through some person digging his toe into him when getting on.

CHAPTER VII

SADDLERY

In this chapter I wish to give a few words on saddlery, the fitting of it, etc.

The Saddle. Take first the saddle; the shape of it depends so much on your style of riding. If you are going to ride in a perfectly ordinary way, with a nice medium length of stirrup, then you want an ordinary plain flap saddle, not cut very far forward, but with sufficient in front of your knee to prevent your breeches getting all dirtied against the muscle of your horse's shoulder when he sweats.

If you are a beginner a very good position for the knee is on the stirrup leather, and this will be obtained by riding with the point of the toe under the knee, that is to say, when you sit up straight and look down you can just see the point of your toe under your knee. Someone will at once say: "That depends if you are riding with the stirrup on the ball of your foot, or right home." It does not matter, it is the stirrup that moves, not the foot.

Fitting the Saddle. The fitting of the

saddle to your horse's back is, I need hardly say, most important; place the saddle on the horse's back in what appears to be the most natural position. How it is going to set depends entirely on the make and shape of your horse, but at any rate you can avoid sore withers and sore backs a great deal, by seeing when you get up on him that you can pass your fingers with plenty of room to spare, between the top of his withers and the saddle, and slip them in behind, between the saddle and his backbone. Try it again when you have been riding for a few minutes, in case the saddle has shifted forward, and thus come down on his withers.

Girths. There is a divided opinion between web and leather girths, at any rate avoid web girths that have been pipe-clayed, because the pipe-clay rots them; grey or brown are good; for myself, I prefer leather girths, I think the rolled girth is the best, but be careful to see that your man keeps it soaped right through.

Girth Tabs. Another point to look to are your girth tabs, by which I mean the straps which are sewn on to the saddle tree for the girths to be buckled to; see that they are kept well soaped, and give a pretty frequent look to their stitching. I mention this because these tabs are under the flap, out of sight, and very often forgotten. I advise the use of Olive Oil soap, you can buy it in bars,

SADDLERY

and I think it is better for your saddlery than those tins of what the stablemen call "fake."

Stirrup Leathers. Keep an eye on your stirrup leathers, you do not want them frightfully thick and clumsy, but they are a bit inclined to get worn where they go through the stirrup if you are always riding the same length.

Altering Stirrups When Mounted. What a lot of people you see who do not know how to alter the length of their stirrups when they are mounted. They take their foot out, drop their reins, put their stick under their arm, pull out the buckle of their stirrup leather and get to work with both hands; whereas, if they would take their reins and stick in one hand, and drop their other hand on to the stirrup leather, which has its buckle close up against the "D" of the saddle, take the end of the stirrup leather in their fingers, pull it up and guide the tongue of the buckle into the hole with the first finger, pressing the strap down with their thumb and steadying the whole thing with their foot, they would make the operation very simple. Or, for letting it down, by taking the strap in the same way, and pulling it up till the tongue is clear of the hole and then pressing with the foot until they have got it to the length they require, pulling the buckle into place by catching hold of the understrap. The right place for the spare end : tuck it underneath the stirrup leather and pull it straight through from behind your leg.

Stirrups. Have your stirrups plenty big enough, so that there is no fear of your foot getting caught in them; see that they are steel—not nickel. If you are showing, take care that your stirrups are big, some judges have very big feet, and if they cannot get their feet into your stirrups, perhaps they will not ride your horse.

Martingales. Use leather martingales, never web. There are different sorts of martingales, we will classify them as standing and running. A standing martingale is generally used on the nose band, that is to say from girth to nose band. It is impossible to lay down the length, but unless you have got a very difficult horse, the best way is to put his head into position, and see that the martingale just touches him. I always think that most standing martingales are made upside down, that is to say, with the buckle so that it comes between the horse's legs. Much better have a nice big loop that your girths can go through, and have the nose band through the buckle end. Another standing martingale has a strap or chain that you can fix to the bit, but this is for the use of the expert, not the beginner.

Running Martingales. These are obliged to have their buckle end on their girth, and are used from the girth on to the reins, that is to say, they are fitted with rings that you can pass the reins through. When using a running martingale on a double bridle, it is best on the rein of the bit, and not on the snaffle, as our forefathers used it. Be sure that you have leather stops on your reins, close up against the bit, if you have at all large rings on the martingale, this to prevent these rings slipping over the rings of the bit, and getting caught up.

There is another martingale I must mention before leaving the subject, which is known as an Irish martingale, and simply consists of a double ring through which the snaffle rein is passed if on a double bridle, or one rein of your snaffle, if you are riding on a snaffle; it is not attached to anything. Another method of attaining the same result is to have a leather loop about four inches long through which you pass all your reins. This is essentially a hunting martingale, and is not of much use for breaking or training, but has a wonderful effect on a horse who is inclined to throw or shake his head.

Bridles. I have already dealt with the most important part of bridles, which is the bit. In " Bitting," you must choose the thickness of reins you like best for yourself, take care that you have a buckle at the end of each rein ; sometimes a horse may get his foot through them, and this little buckle may save you a lot of trouble. The reins and head piece should be stitched on to the bit, buckles are ugly, studs unsafe, but always keep a good buckle bridle, it is very useful when you wish to try another bit on your horse.

Nose Band. This should be entirely separate from the bridle, with a head strap of its own, which is passed through the loops of the brow band, the reason for this is, it prevents your bridle from coming off if you have a fall. Rather a good rule for fitting a nose band is, that it should lie two fingers' breadth below a horse's cheek-bone, the tightness of it I leave to you. I have already mentioned it in bitting. The breadth is a matter of taste, a nice wide nose band furnishes your horse's face, but a very wide nose band is vulgar.

Curb Chain. Use a nice medium weight curb chain, thin ones cut and break, very thick ones are too heavy. Curb straps are very nice, and should be used on good-mouthed horses a great deal more than they are.

Curb Straps. A curb strap is a flat strap, fitted with three links at each end, and a link for the lip strap. I venture to say that if these were more frequently used there would be fewer, so called, bad-mouthed horses.

Let me here again call your attention to the very important suggestion on how to put a curb chain on a Pelham bridle, given earlier in the chapter on Bitting.

Lip Strap. As I stated in the chapter on Bitting, lip straps should always be used on a double bridle or Pelham.

Brow Band. Plain leather, *only coloured* when showing a hack; they are otherwise used by dealers as a trade-mark on hirelings.

CHAPTER VIII

SHOWING

I do not for one instant suppose that the showing fraternity will find anything that is of much interest to them in this chapter; if they do, so much the better; it is written with a view to helping the novice who goes showing. Somebody, who has perhaps a nice hunter, or a pony to show in the hack class, and who really would stand a very good chance among the competitors, but not knowing anything about the game does not know how to present their steed or how it should be ridden, and there is not the least doubt that unless a horse is properly presented and well ridden, he is very likely to get passed over by the judges.

Points of a Show Horse. Let me try and explain what I mean by presenting the horse. First of all he must be in good condition, nice and round but at the same time fit, you can well afford to have your hunter with a little bit more meat on him in the summer, than he would have when in hard hunting condition. It is no good bringing a blemished horse into the show ring. I mean by blemished, a chipped or slightly enlarged knee, a spavin, or curb, or a blind eye. Your horse must be to all intents and purposes sound. What is a good show horse? The horse that wins the class should be, in the judges' opinion, the nearest to perfection, complying with the requirements of that class. That is to say: it is no good putting a fourteen stone hunter into a class that is laid down for thirteen stone horses, or vice versa, a light weight horse in a heavy weight class, because, good though he may be, he does not comply with the conditions of the class.

Action and Manners. The show horse must be true of action, that is to say, when he is run in hand, he must move straight, he must be a good walker, and he must be able to use himself in his gallop, if he is going into a hunter class. His manners must be good, he must stand still to let the judge get on and off; manners are more important in a hack class than they are in a hunter class, but at the same time, in the hunter class if a horse plays up in the ring, and shows bad manners, it is not every judge that is going to take the trouble to ride him.

A day's judging is a very tiring thing. I once heard a well-known judge say to an exhibitor with a very nice-looking horse that was mad fresh, and had been bucking with his owner, when the owner asked him why he did not ride his horse, "I have come here, sir, to judge horses, not for a day's Broncho busting," and so the horse which most of us thought was one of the best-looking in the class, stood at the bottom.

Exercise. Give your horse plenty of exercise on the morning of a show. I do not want to bring anything personal into this chapter, but I attributed a great deal of my success in showing, to the fact that I was always on the show ground at dawn to superintend the working of my horses. A statement that any stud groom or show man of those days will bear out. You may say, "Why so early?" Because your horse must be perfectly dressed, not a hair out of place, when he goes into the ring.

"Dressing" the Horse. If he has a mane, it must be nicely plaited, with seven big plaits, one forelock, six down crest; if you are a novice, and your man does not understand the art of mane plaiting, there are always one or two old chaps who follow the shows who will do anything, let alone plait a mane, for a very trifling consideration.

The tail must be nicely pulled, and just before going into the ring, put a little paraffin in the palm of your hands and run them down the tail; a nice shine and the hair keeps in place.

When you are up on his back waiting to go into the ring, have him rubbed over with a very soft rubber. These are little points but every little tells.

Show Saddlery. Then, as to saddlery; no martingale, never a martingale in a hack or hunter class : if your horse is not sufficiently broken for you to ride him without one, he is not fit to be shown.

The saddle should be put two inches further back than you ever dreamt of having it before; if he has got a good shoulder you will give him a bit more, if he has a bad shoulder you are improving it.

A showing saddle should have a little bit of velvet stitched in it, to go each side of the withers, with the nap of the velvet against the coat, this will keep the saddle back.

Your bridle carefully cleaned, never a snaffle bridle (I am not talking about jumpers which is an art all its own), the head piece of the bridle should for a few days before have been cleaned like your brown shoes. A coloured brow band, as I have said before, *in a hack class only*. The reins nicely soaped, never polished, boot polish is nasty stuff on the hands; your steel glittering. Now the judge will say: "There is one properly turned out, at any rate."

Show Riding. The whole of your attention should be fixed on what you are doing, and that from the time you go through the gate into the ring, until the ribbon is hanging on your brow band. Do not keep looking around for your friends, or thinking about something other than the job you have in hand, you need not keep a fixed stare on the judge, you are sure to be going to walk round two or three times, a most important moment, believe me, because the judge's first impression very often goes a long way.

I am not going to pretend that when you become more of an adept at the art, you will not watch the judge a bit out of the tail of your eye, to try and glean what that first impression is, but brother beginner, what you have got to do is : to sit up, and look up, with your hands down, your horse's head nicely placed, and try and make him walk out with a nice loose rein.

You will then be told to trot round, if it is a hunter class, a nice steady trot, riding him with your legs all the time to make him put his foot well out. Why I say ride him with your legs to make him put his foot out is because, sometimes when you get a horse into a ring, even when he has been moving well in his trot at home, he is looking at the crowd, and though you may not realise it, he has shortened his pace by several inches. A hunter should move nice and straight and true, but not with the extravagant action of a hack.

Hacks Trotting. If you are showing a hack, you want to sharpen your trot, I do not mean dash round like a Hackney, but ride your horse, lifting him a little with the bridle to make him lift his foot and bend his knee, riding him with your legs to make him lengthen his pace.

The way I used to train my hacks (I am sorry this is a personal note again, but I cannot help it) was to count to them one, two, three, four, gradually raising and sharpening my voice till they got worked right up to the required pace, and I may often have been heard in the ring counting under my breath.

All this time you will have been sitting right back in your saddle, exposing that wonderful front, perhaps even running your hand down his mane to show how far you are from his ears.

The best trained horse in the world may with the band playing, and the crowd round the ring, break his trot, you should have prepared him for this while you were training him. Have a signal that he knows, a low whistle, or say in an undertone " OOH trot." Another very good way to make a horse that has broken settle down into his trot is to run your hand down his mane, two fingers each side. Old Jack Goodwin taught me that and I think he knew as much about showing as any man I ever met.

Galloping Hunters. You will then be told, if it is a hunter class, to "gallop on"; don't lurch forward and loose your reins and start to gallop, sit down on the back of your saddle, with your hands crammed down, lift him into a canter, and gradually increase it to what you know or consider to be your horse's best pace.

Having trained him on the lines laid down in the early chapters of this book, and he therefore being perfectly balanced, you need have no fears of the corners, you can go round them as fast as you like.

A very good way with a show hunter, is to have a screw hole left on the outside of the heel of each shoe, which you fill with a piece of tow, and if when you get to the show, you think the ring is going to be very greasy, then screw in a stud, usually one in each hind foot is sufficient, and see for yourself that they are taken out the minute he comes out of the ring.

Cantering Hacks. If you are showing a hack you will be told to "canter on," you will draw him back slightly, and lift him in that dead slow, oily canter, beloved of the hack man. Sit up and sit still, and show that your seat is like sitting in an arm-chair.

Watch The Judge. In both cases, hack and hunter, this is the time to begin to keep an eye open for a signal from the steward or the judge to come into the centre. Do not shorten your circle, or when you are called in, come dashing into the middle, pushing for the top place, it is vulgar, come in quietly, if you are called in first you will do well to get fairly close up to the *jump*, because it is nice to stand at the top, and if you leave too much space, one of the push and cut division will chance a reprimand from the ring steward and pull in above you.

Do not think because you have been called in that your job is done, and relax all your muscles and let your horse go to sleep, resting one foot; only half your job is done. If you are standing at the top, or nearly there, you have got to stay there, if you are lower down you have got to get there, so jump off and put your horse on his legs and keep him there looking all alert, because you never know when the judges, while calling in the rest of the class, may glance in your direction.

Etiquette in the Ring. The judges will then come round and have a look at your horse, do not try to hold an affable conversation with them on the weather or any other topic, they are busy, if they ask you any questions, answer shortly and then hold your tongue, all the time concentrate on your horse, perhaps just playing with his bit, anything to make him present himself at his best. A little bit of grass may be hidden in the palm of the hand just to make him keep his head up and ears cocked. If the judge wants to feel a hind leg, pick up a fore foot, because you will go right out in the betting if he kicks one of the judges, and now is the time, when they have passed on a couple of horses down the line, to relax—you should be aching if you have done what I have told you.

However, do not go to sleep, keep your eye open for the judge coming back to have a ride. When he says he will ride your horse, go round to the off side, hold the stirrup, offer him your little stick to balance himself with, and be ready to take your horse when he comes back. Do not let your desire to be affable get the better of you, hold your tongue.

"Saddles Off." When the judges have finished riding, you will be told to take your saddle off; a good way is always to loose your girths when both judges have ridden, to give your horse a breather. The minute you are told to take your saddle off, slide it off quickly, being careful not to ruffle his coat more than you can help, and if you have got a chance wipe the saddle mark away with your handkerchief, take your reins over his head, end of the reins in your left hand, your right hand holding them close up to the bit.

Now wait till you are called out; when you get the signal, lead your horse out and stand him against the side of the ring, stand in front of him to make him show himself to the best advantage.

Running in Hand. You must be very careful before taking your horse to a show, to teach him to run in hand, because nothing is more horrible than to see a horse jogging along behind his master, or on the other hand being towed. Teach him to jog slowly with you running beside his shoulder, right hand holding the reins close up to the bit, the end of the reins in your left hand. Do not slop along yourself, run smartly in step with your horse, this is very important; when you turn round, turn your horse away from you to keep him balanced. I venture to say that a good display in hand has turned the scale in many a class. Now go back and put your saddle on, put it well back, you may be called upon to give another display if the judges have not decided, or should a referee have to be called in, wait until you hear your fate, and brother beginner, whatever it is, *meet it with a smile*.

How to Accept the Verdict. It is a horrid feeling when you are moved down, it is a glorious feeling when you are moved up, whichever it is, smile and remember that you have put your horse into the hands of these men to judge. You hope they have done their best without prejudice, and whether they have or not you have got to accept it, so you may as well smile.

If you become a Judge. I will, however, say this to you, brother beginner, if you in your turn come to be a judge, do not consider that the person whose horse you are judging, because he has brought his horse into the ring to be judged by you, is a vastly inferior person to yourself and knows nothing; remember he has bought that horse, and perhaps many others, and maybe he knows a great deal more than you do. If you have put him down, don't go up to him when he is feeling sore, but being a thoroughly good sportsman not showing it, and make some stupid remark as to the reason why you put his horse down, he is not in a position to reply to you; and very often you have that loophole of escape, by saying that you have ridden the other horses and very likely he has not.

Show Equipment. Just one more word, take care that you go to the show well equipped. I mean with everything you may require for tying your horse up, a bucket for watering him, the necessary grooming materials, etc., for though the show world is as a rule kind, it does not want to keep on lending; on the other hand, beware of the sharp-fingered fraternity generally represented at most meetings, who *borrow* and return not again.

CHAPTER IX

CHILDREN'S PONIES

Some people will very likely say, "What does this fellow know about children's ponies?" My reply is, "As much as most people, and more than some," because when I was round the country buying horses, or at any time when I saw a good child's pony, I always bought it. I generally knew somebody who wanted one, and if I did not, I could be quite sure that I should be asked for one in the near future.

I look upon the choosing of the correct type of children's ponies as being one of the most important things to do with education in the upbringing of the future generation.

The Wrong Method. It is iniquitous to put children up on the horrible bad mouthed unbroken or badly broken ponies that you so often see them endeavouring to ride. You break their nerve from the start. How many of the hundreds of children that start riding every year, do you think are made to dread that daily ride? I am afraid if you were to go into statistics, a surprisingly large per cent. would be found, and only because they are put upon a pony of which they have not the least control. They start by feeling helpless and that the task in front of them is hopeless, let alone being afraid of the pony running away with them or throwing them off.

Do not think, because you do not mind your horse playing up that everybody is the same, and especially little children. I do not wish to bring them up soft—far from it—but I want them brought on gradually.

You remember the old theory, that if you threw a child into the deep end of the swimming bath, it would swim, well, it did not; instead of teaching it to swim, if you did not drown it, you very likely gave it a hatred of water for life, so be careful not to do the same by putting a little boy or girl on a pony which they cannot manage.

I love to teach young things, and my method has always been, never mind what the subject, to set them the easiest of tasks, which they can master without the least doubt and gradually bring them on, and this I venture to say, means more in riding perhaps than anything.

The First Pony. If you can find a narrow old pony, or a narrow pony that is perfectly quiet, never mind if he is a little bigger than you thought was the right size, but so be it that his manners are perfect, that is my ideal pony to start a child on, and in the meantime you can be on the look-out for a better one and one that can be trained. The great difficulty about these very small ponies is, that in many cases nobody has ever been able to ride them and properly break them. There is no reason, if you will study my chapters on mouthing and long rein driving, why you should not break your pony to all that is laid down in them, and if you look about, you can generally find some undersized lad who will ride them under your supervision until they are fit to carry the little beginner.

Feeding and Exercising. I do not think a children's pony should ever be given corn until the child is old enough to take it out hunting, then, and then only, a little corn may be necessary. The old coachman of the past generation has, I regret to say, become nearly extinct; I regret chiefly, because it means that horses are being used less and less, but at the same time, that old man, who stuffed his carriage horses with hard corn, ruined many a budding horseman and horsewoman, because he overfed the children's ponies.

Plenty of exercise should be the rule for children's ponies; they are the hardiest little beasts in the world, and can always be led alongside a horse, or driven in a governess cart, put to mow, or roll the lawn—anything for exercise.

Shetland Ponies. I do not like Shetland ponies for children, and apologise to the Shetland breeders for this statement. It may be that I have had unfortunate experience with them, but I do not think that the breed is docile, and as they age they get too broad in the back.

Teaching. I have said, teach gradually; a great deal, however, depends on the age of the child, but take your child of six or seven, and we will assume you have bought that quiet pony, put a comfortable saddle on it, not one of those dreadful saddles that we see sold as children's saddles; go to any good saddler, and ask them to try and find you a little old polo saddle; do not start a child on a new saddle, it is not fair.

Gymnastics. Now you will start walking away beside the pony, and as things go on, riding beside it; but from the very beginning, every day a few exercises for two or three minutes, such as, hands above the head, down, and touch the toes, lay back head touching the croup, up again, without catching hold of anything. A little help may be necessary at first, but soon the child will be able to carry on by itself. Let the youngster climb about all over the pony, sit the wrong way round, in fact do anything; all this tends, not only to supple and develop the child, but to give that lithe and easy seat, by which you can tell a well-taught horseman or horsewoman, all the world over.

Progressive Education. Another thing is our progressive education; try and teach one fact every day, such as: "A horse only breathes through its nostrils": then the next day ask, "What did I tell you about a horse's breathing yesterday?" or, "What did we say about such and such a thing the day before?" Think what a lot of knowledgeable little facts about a horse, saddlery, stable management, etc., you can put into that receptive young mind in a year.

Free Riding. Let us now conclude that you have come to the stage when the leading rein can be dispensed with, and you go hacking along together, add to your few minutes physical exercises, a few minutes free riding, by free riding, I mean, you get into a field or some open space, and your pupil rides the pony round about, while you sit in the middle, thus teaching them to control the pony, turn it, and make it go where they wish.

When he has arrived at doing this, and your pupil is able to get up and down himself, alter the length of the stirrups in the correct way, and tighten the girths, your little horseman will be getting on with his education, and if your pony can jump, you can then start him over a very low obstacle.

Choosing a Pony. I consider that a first-class children's pony is worth anything ; what can it matter, that you spend twenty or thirty pounds extra, if you are going to lay the foundation of another first-class horseman or horsewoman.

I have seen some rotten judging in the show ring in my time, but I have always been able to reconcile myself by saying : " Well, perhaps, it was a wonderful ride, or perhaps it was this, that, or the other," but the worst judging I have ever seen and have never been able to reconcile myself to, is, when a bad-mannered, fractious, good-looking, beautifully-made pony, which is three parts out of control, is put first in a children's pony class. I recall, as if it were yesterday, a pony that reared over backwards in the ring, being put first in the children's pony class at the International Horse Show.

Paces, and manners ; then make, and shape, when you are judging children's ponies, please.

I bought a pony from my old friend, Mr. Maxwell Angus, in this fashion. I went over to his place in Ireland one day, to see if he happened to have anything in my line, and we drove round the farm in an outside car ; his little daughter accompanied us, riding an odd spotted pony. She opened the gates for us, and when we got into the field with a lot of colts, she rounded them up close to the outside car. I had no eyes for the colts ; my whole attention was fixed on this wonderful pony in his little single rein bridle, and the perfect display that he and his rider were giving.

I said to Mr. Maxwell Angus: "How much for the pony, Max?" He said: "I could not sell him till my little girl outgrows him, or when she goes to school." I said: "All right, how much?" and he told me. I said: "It is a deal. I will give you a cheque when we get into the house, and you send me the pony, not when *you* have finished with him (for although he was only, I think I am right in saying, about 13.3, Mr Angus used to ride him himself), but when your little girl has finished with him." I gave him the cheque and the address to send the pony to, and I think it was 18 months before that pony, which I considered to be one of the best children's ponies that I ever saw, went to his new home, where he is still.

Side Saddle or Cross Saddle. Before I leave the subject I want to say a word on the question of riding astride for little girls. This must form part of the early lesson, but how often one sees them put on wide-backed ponies, or even horses, with rough paces and bad saddles; surely it must be wrong. I know that it is very handy and almost necessary in these times for ladies to be able to ride astride as well as side saddle, but I implore of you let all girls be taught side saddle chiefly; if there must be astride riding, then see to it that only a really narrow backed pony is used. We poor males were made flat inside the thigh to fit a saddle but women were not. I once heard it said by a great authority that in his opinion many of the troubles of girls and women in after life were caused by riding astride too much when they were young. Not only that, but what is more beautiful than a woman who can ride, mounted side saddle on a good horse? I have yet to see one astride who looks as well. Another thing, once up on a side saddle what a tremendously firm seat they have got, and it is to this grip, more than to their lightness of touch, that I attribute the fact that you so often find women with the best of hands.

In the old days they were rather encumbered by their habit skirts, but in these days of apron skirts a woman can get up and down with ease. There is no need for a girl to have skirts if she has a good astride kit, with a nice long coat, she can ride side saddle in it without a skirt or apron perfectly well. Some lady reading this may say: "It's all very well for him to talk, but what does he know of side saddle?" "My reply is, Madam, I schooled all my horses side saddle myself before anyone else was allowed to ride them that way." I hope shortly to institute side saddle classes at many Shows, and also prizes for turn out.

CHAPTER X

WHEN BUYING A HORSE—A FEW THINGS TO REMEMBER

Buying a horse is a very difficult thing. You are very often up against people whose business it is to make their livelihood, in some measure at least, out of the uninitiated, and even if you are not a novice, there are a great many things to consider. First of all you must not take it for granted that you know what you want.

Conformation and Type. I used always to divide this very difficult question into two parts. The first, conformation; the second, is the horse a good ride, or likely to make a good ride, that is if he was already broken? Conformation also bears greatly on whether he is going to make a good ride or not.

Know What You Want. As I said in my foreword, you go into a dealer's yard and you get all flustered. When the horse is brought out your first look gives you a general impression. It may not be the sort of horse you want, but we will take it for granted that it is. Then, is he up to your weight? That does not only refer to the amount of bone he has below the knee, but to his general conformation, and above all, his back and loins.

I am not going into every detail of what a horse should be, but I am going to give you a few points that must be considered.

Begin at the Ground. I was once told by an old sportsman: "When you are buying a horse, begin at the ground."

Foreleg. We will therefore follow that good advice and start at the ground. See that he has good feet, a nice foreleg, with no lumps and bumps about his joints. A good way to ascertain roughly how much bone he has, is to measure below the knee by putting your hand round the limb; the finger and thumb of an average hand will very nearly encircle eight inches, and eight inches of good bone should carry anything. Always remember that flat bone is preferable to round.

Knees and Splints. Now have a good look at his knees, because it is easy for an artist to conceal chipped knees, and a horse with marked knees has lost a very great deal of his value. Running your hand down his leg you will probably find a splint, and if it is a good big well-developed one it should not worry him. Run your finger and thumb down the back of his leg and see that the tendon is straight, not bowed, and does not show any signs of having been doctored.

When Buying A Horse

You will say that these are a great many points to remember in so small a portion of so large an animal, but I always think that the knee to the hoof and the hock to the hoof are very vulnerable parts of a horse.

Hindleg and Curb. Next the hindleg, a nice straight hindleg, not one of the sickle variety; the chief thing to look for is a curb. The curb is an enlargement of the bone just below the hock or on the hock, and it is easily detected by running your first finger firmly down the back of the hock, and if you feel an enlargement in the middle of the bone you are pretty certain that it is a curb. I say the middle of the bone, as some horses' hock bones protrude a little on each side of the seat of the curb.

The wise man when handling a strange horse's hindleg will get the person who is holding him to pick up a forefoot.

Spavins and Thoroughpins. Such things as spavins and thoroughpins we must leave for your Veterinary Surgeon to discover, if you decide on buying him, for if a horse is worth having and you are a novice, he is certainly worth a Veterinary Surgeon's examination.

General Appearance. Now let us take his general conformation: a big honest eye (a rough test of eyesight is just to pass your hand in front of the horse's eye, about two or three inches away, if the eye flickers he is at any rate not blind; your Veterinary Surgeon must do the rest), a nicely set on head and neck, a good back and a deep heart. I always used to stand back and see that the depth from the top of his withers to the bottom of girth was about equal to the distance from his elbow to his shoe. You will find many horses with a slight hollow underneath where the girth will go, and by the position of this hollow you can tell at once how he is going to carry his saddle. The further back the hollow, the better he will carry the saddle. My old friend and adviser, Captain Wenty Hope Johnson, from whom as a boy I acquired much knowledge, gave me this tip and I have found it well-nigh infallible. I have also found that very few people know it.

Back Rib to Hip. See that the ribs are deep and well sprung, that is to say, do not buy a horse which looks like a drain-pipe. Another good measurement to know, is, just the width of your four fingers in between his back rib and his hip bone, that is what is known as being well ribbed up. If you find a horse with a long distance between his rib and his hip bone he is likely to be slack of his back and weak of his loin and a difficult horse to keep in condition.

Cavity under Tail. Having looked at him sideways, stand in front of him, he should be nice and wide between the eyes, plenty of room between his forelegs; now go round behind him, see that he does not turn his hocks in, have his forefoot lifted up and look under his tail. Believe me, I have turned down many a horse that I thought I should buy, when I have looked under his tail and found a sunken cavity big enough to put my fist into. You will generally find that a horse with that cavity is split right up behind, both are signs of weakness, and I venture to say that ninety per cent. of the horses that are sunken behind are bad doers and bad stayers. This does not always apply to a mare, you can forgive a small cavity if she is not split up.

Pace and Action. Now have your horse walked up twenty or thirty yards, stand aside and look at his side view, now stand in front of him and see if he moves straight and true, coming to you and going from you, does not turn his front toes in or out, and does not throw either or both of his feet; by throwing I mean showing the sole of his foot to the side, this is called dishing, you will see it best when he has gone past you. There are many ways of concealing a horse turning his foot by special shoeing, but I think a very good way of making certain if the foot is put on right is by picking it up and seeing that the point of the frog is perfectly straight.

Now have him trotted up; see if he is

sound, and you may find that the horse you have not detected as going crooked in his walk, will show this at once when he trots.

Height. My advice to a novice, unless you have some special reason for buying a very big horse, is to buy a horse of 15.2 or 15.3 hands high. I think the war proved to us all that the small horse could kill the big horse, and that he could live on a ration which was starvation diet to the big horse.

Age. You will have asked or been told his age. I am not going into the question here of teeth markings, the most knowledgeable may so easily be deceived, as the faking of teeth has been brought to a fine art, but even if they are not faked, the teeth of a four-year-old who has been well fed on hard corn may easily make him out to be a year older than his real age. I once showed a home-bred four-year-old, I had foaled his mother down myself, the judge looked at him and said he was a five-year-old. I said he was not, they called in a vet., who also said he was a five-year-old. I, however, referred them to the National Pony Stud Book in which the pony was entered. You can only go by the mouth and the horse in general. The cavity over the eye gets deeper as the horse ages. It is a difficult thing to say at what age he is at his prime, this so entirely depends on how he has been treated as a youngster, but foreign nations consider a horse to be of full value at an age when in England he would be considered old.

See Saddle put on. Now you can intimate that you would like to see a saddle on him. My advice is, see that saddle put on. I am not a believer in a horse being taken away round a corner out of sight to be saddled up, and a man reappearing riding him.

You may think I am very distrustful, but it is not so much that, as that when you see a horse saddled, you at any rate know that his back is all right, for if it is not he will either go down behind when the saddle is put on him, or when the dealer's man gets on him.

Weak Back. Do not necessarily take it for granted, because a horse shrinks a bit when a cold saddle is put on, that he is wrong in the back ; he may feel rather the same as you would if somebody suddenly clapped something cold in the middle of your back ; but what I do not like to see is a horse that goes down, and then, when somebody gets on to him, crouches and rather drags his hind legs for the first few strides. That is one thing you look out for when you see the horse saddled ; there are of course many others. Many horses will round their backs, but very often that is nothing.

See Horse Ridden. Next see him ridden ; pay particular attention to the way he goes away from his stable, or the direction of his stable, because you do not want to buy a confirmed nappy one. Having satisfied yourself that he goes away comfortably, you will see him put through his paces, and then over a very small fence or two, and thus you will decide by his general deportment, whether this is the horse you want.

Mount and Try Horse Yourself. Then get up and ride him yourself. Brother beginner, two points—first, never get up and ride until you have seen someone else ride the horse; second, when you are mounting him stand alongside his shoulder, facing his tail, and swing up from there, not only is it the proper way to mount at all times, but if you stand facing the saddle, and put your foot in the stirrup, you may just touch his side with your toes, and the effect of that on some half-broken horse is rather like an earthquake. When you are on top you will at once see what his front is like, take a look round, and see what he is like behind, then put him through his paces gently. Do not act as I have seen so many people do, who have come to buy a horse from me, that is to catch hold of him by the head and put him to a gallop, because, not only will you by this method discover little or nothing about him, but your friend the dealer will at once know that you know nothing. As I say, try him gently, turning him both ways, taking

When Buying A Horse

him as near to his stable as you can, and riding him away from it, and be sure before you get off him, that you have backed him a few strides. The reason you do that is to test his back, and now I leave you to complete the deal.

Price. A good general principle to remember that whoever you are buying the horse from, is almost sure to ask a little more than he expects to get.

Do not forget to give the dealer's man a little bit, in case you go to him to buy another horse at any time. It is very often a good thing to have a friend at court. Many a time I have heard it said, " Oh, no, Sir, do not show Mr. So-and-so, that one, he is a nice gentleman " ; and that invariably means that Mr. So-and-so has not forgotten to tip the dealer's man.

CHAPTER XI

RIDING KIT—HOW TO DRESS

Riding Kit. Sometimes it may happen that one takes to riding quite late in life; perhaps has made enough money to be able to afford that greatest of pleasures, which has been debarred earlier, owing to the bank balance not being quite firm enough.; or perhaps a medical adviser orders horse exercise, at any rate, you desire to ride, or that your son or daughter shall ride, and at once there arises the question of clothes.

You have no previous experience, and the only way out of the difficulty is to ask your tailor, or some other tailor, who advertises himself as " Ladies' and Gent's Sporting Outfitters," or the like. Probably he does not really know, he has only picked up his ideas from other tailors, or from seeing people wrongly dressed on hirelings at the seaside during his annual holiday, so he advises as best he can, at the same time with an eye to stuffing into you as much as he can.

May I therefore give a few words of advice on the subject. First of all you are going to learn to ride, and you want comfort and ease, not to guy yourself up like a hog in armour, in corduroys, etc.

Of course I must leave colour of materials to you, but nothing looks nicer than a grey riding suit, or buff-brown breeches, with a grey coat and waistcoat. Choose a good stout material, with a bit of wear in it, not too thick or too stiff, a good Chipping Norton cord, such as our fathers wore, is as good as anything, but nowadays there are plenty of good materials to choose from.

Breeches. Have your breeches cut nice and full in the seat, with plenty of room over the hips, clean under the knee, and the knee buttons so that they button just on the inside of your shin bone. Our forefathers wore both breeches and gaiters to button down the outside, but we do not, we wear them inside. In the old days the tailor used to put his finger into that little hollow just below, and to the right or left of your knee-cap, and put the first button of his breeches there, but as I say, we don't; we bring the buttons over to the other side of the shin bone, and therefore the breeches must be built to be worn like that. When you try them on, be sure there is no wrinkle between the buttons, and that you bend your knee with comfort; also that you have plenty of room underneath, so that when you raise your foot to place it in the stirrup for mounting, your breeches do not drag over your posterior, and along the back muscles of your thigh.

Continuations. Good breeches do not need continuations, they are uncomfortable things and the buttons run into your legs, but if you must have them, then let the buttons run down outside the shin bone, and do not blame me if they hurt.

Buckskin strappings wear better than strappings of the same material as the breeches.

I think a belt is more comfortable than braces for riding.

Buttons at the knee are preferable to laces.

Leg and Foot Wear. It is for you to choose if you will wear boots and gaiters, or jack boots. If boots and gaiters then wear lace boots, nice and high in the leg (black for choice), and let the opening of your gaiter (brown for choice), fasten down the same line as your breeches buttons. If you decide on boots, then have black or brown; semi-stiff legs are the most comfortable and best wearing. With boots you must wear a garter strap, and do not forget the place for the buckle is in the front of your leg, right in the middle, just touching the breeches buttons, the strap going in between the third and fourth button. A golden rule is, in boots you show four buttons, in gaiters, three only.

Spurs. Spurs are not necessary, but if worn, take care that they are well up to your ankle bone, and have spur rests on your boots; nothing looks so horrid as a drooping spur. See that the bottom straps are long enough for the spur to lie absolutely level. So much for the covering of your lower limbs.

Coat and Waistcoat. Now a nice coat and waistcoat, single breasted of course, coat cut nice and long; a very good idea of length is to hold your arm straight down, fingers extended and let the tips of the fingers be the length of the coat. A single slit up the back, twelve to fourteen inches, and a nice full skirt, cut forward; if you do this you will not find yourself sitting on your coat every time you meet your saddle.

Neck Wear. For hacking, you will find your ordinary collar and tie the most comfortable, and my advice to you is: the first few times you go out hunting, go in your comfortable hacking kit, and study what the right people wear; you need not fear being out of place, or wrongly dressed, if you wear what I have described.

Head Gear. As regards head dress, in the country, a cap or soft hat; in the Row, a bowler, white in summer. No, no hat guard, and remember a short cane or stick, no hunting crop or cutting whip; in the former the thong only adds to your difficulties, and without a thong is wrong always; the latter only for experts, racing or polo. Your little stick should be 24 to 32 inches long, quite plain ash cane, or anything plain.

Pin or safety pin, in tie or stock, horizontal; if vertical, it would go into you if you had a fall.

Gloves, large and comfortable, dogskin for choice, knitted string in wet weather.

If you are a female (or have to dress a female), riding astride, dress as men, but with a longer coat; if for side saddle, a nice grey, blue, or brown habit, with a collar and tie, or soft shirt and collar, and a comfortable hat.

CHAPTER XII

MISCELLANEOUS DO'S AND DON'T'S!

If your horse is in a stall, turn him round before you girth up, or you will strain the tree of your saddle.

A good way, especially with a cold-backed horse, is to put your saddle on half-an-hour before you go out. Do not girth it up till you are ready to start; you can throw your clothing over the horse on top of the saddle.

Don't leave your horse loose in a box with his saddle on, or he will roll and break the tree.

It is a good thing to leave a horse loose in his box for three or four minutes after he comes in, before you put the clothing on, so that he may relieve himself and enjoy a roll, but do not leave him long enough to get chilled.

Don't trot the moment you get your horse away from the stable, unless you are fetching a fire engine, or the Doctor, or have some like important business; let your horse walk for a bit, then jog quietly on.

Do not bring your horse in sweating if you

can possibly help it; walk him for the last quarter of a mile, so that he comes in cool.

If you have a horse that is in the habit of breaking out into a cold sweat, after he is done wipe him over with a moist sponge, not wet. Don't give him a bath, but just damp, and then lead him about in the fresh air for a few minutes.

See that his ears are dry and warm.

Never sit on your horse's back unnecessarily; if you are having a long day hunting or anything else, the minute there is a check, or you have an opportunity, jump off; if he is blowing and there is time, loose your girths (don't forget to tighten them again before you get on), but even if there is not time to loosen your girths, jump off and raise the back of your saddle; it will freshen his back, and getting off will freshen you.

Don't look at your horse when you are leading him; some people get in front of their horse and look at him as they are leading him in and out of the stable; just get in front of him and let him follow you.

A good way, if you are boxing a horse, and he will not go into the box, is to let somebody lead him, and get the porter to get behind him on one side, and you get behind him on the other, clasp hands low down behind his quarters, and lift him in. No, you will not get kicked, you are too close to him. If you are loading a lot of mules or troop horses, this

Miscellaneous Do's and Don't's! 123

is a better method than all whips, and do not have a crowd of people standing round, only just the three of you; a crowd of people only makes the animal think that something awful is going to happen.

If you have got a horse that is difficult in a horse box, do not tie him up, but pass the rope, which is attached to his head collar, through into the compartment, and let a lad hold it.

If the horse is travelling alone he must take his chance, but with a valuable horse you do not know, it is well worth the extra fare, to send somebody with him.

Don't jerk your horse in the mouth when leading him, it is a favourite form of punishment by some grooms and bad stablemen, who, through their own carelessness, have let the horse tread on their foot, or something has startled him, and he receives a job in the mouth that conveys nothing intelligible to him and ruins him for leading.

Don't believe good hands are born, not made; the foundation of making good hands is the position of hands and elbows (see Mouthing), and a firm seat.

Don't forget when training your horse to accustom him to a whip or a stick being swung round his head. Start by doing it very gently, a good way to start is to whistle a tune, and beat time. A horse has a wonderful ear for music, and the rhythm of a tune, like " The

Merry Widow" waltz, whistled quietly, will very often soothe him when he is all upset, and I think the reason of this very often is that you are edgy, and that the mere fact of whistling the quiet tune, has, without your knowing it, made you relax your muscles. I mention "The Merry Widow" waltz, because that tune has a most extraordinarily soothing effect on all animals; I have proved it with horses; I have proved it when I have been training a cockerel for the show bench, and I have an old parrot who will do anything when I whistle that tune to her.

I heard a man say once that he never went out hacking without learning something; it is true.

When you are out hacking, never mind if you are riding the best broken hack in the world, rein him back a few times during the ride; in the same way, if he is a properly broken horse let him passage once to the right and left, and if he does not do it perfectly make him do it again until he does. Horses, like ourselves, soon become slack, and easily get into the habit of doing a thing wrong, unless careful attention is paid.

If you have a horse with a "dickey" tendon, a strip of inner tube inside the bandage, makes a fine support.

A piece of inner tube makes a wonderful brushing boot, better than felt, because the dust does not get into it, and when you come

Miscellaneous Do's and Don't's! 125

in, you sponge it over, and it is as good as new. By the way, brother beginner, you put a brushing boot on a horse who hits his fetlock joints; this is generally caused by weakness, sometimes by bad shoeing. If it is weakness, it can be remedied by the shoe being slightly bevelled on the inside of the foot that is hitting.

Two Secrets.—No. 1. If you have got a filled tendon, instead of buying those very expensive little pots of paste, take a bowl, and make yourself a paste, half vinegar, half methylated spirit, and either flour or powdered chalk. Put this paste on the tendon, then envelop the leg in cotton wool, or better still what I think is called, gamgee tissue (I mean wadding that is sold in layers), then put your bandage on.

No. 2. A lotion for bringing down lumps and bumps. Mark you this for your knees, ye members of the jumping fraternity; two thirds lead lotion, one third methylated spirit, and an equal part of water.

Use iodine and water freely for cuts and abrasions; salt and water, for a tender back.

It is a common idea that a horse's hide is much less vulnerable than our own skin; it is not, it is just twice as vulnerable; a lotion that *you* can rub on a sprained ankle or knee, will blister a horse.

Do not clip a horse's ears out, it may be smart, but the hair was put there for the purpose of keeping out flies and insects, so take a pair of scissors and trim the ears flush. A horse may give you a very nasty ride if he gets a fly in his ear, for it drives him nearly mad, in fact I have seen a mare go quite mad from this cause.

If you are going to turn a hog maned horse out to grass let him have at any rate, a few days growth of mane as a protection, if there is likely to be any sun.

Do not groom your horse for a few days before turning him out, the grease in his coat is a protection against the weather.

Do not get all hot and bothered if when you catch a youngster up out of the field, you find he is full of lice, rather rejoice for it is said to be a sign that he is full blooded and in good health. The cure is to sponge him all over with a wash, composed of one third ordinary paraffin and two thirds water or a slightly stronger mixture if necessary. The sponging must be thorough to be effective, and be repeated as found necessary.

If you are riding a gelding, and you hear a funny noise like the squelching of water, put your hand up and draw his sheath gently down and apply a little pure vaseline.

Be careful never to girth your horse up suddenly; tighten your girths moderately before mounting, and then when you have been out for a few minutes, you will probably be able to take them up another couple of holes. No, brother beginner, do not kick your foot out of the stirrup and bring your leg back behind the saddle as you will see a lot of people do, who do not know any better, but keep your foot in the stirrup; hitch your knee up a little; put your hand under the flap of your saddle from behind; pull up your girth, guiding the tongue of the buckle into the hole with the first finger; now if your horse gives a start forward your leg will drop into position, but had you been doing it the other way you would probably be biting the dust.

If your stirrup leathers are too long, don't cut the ends off; take them to the saddler and have the buckle end shortened. This applies to all saddlery and straps.

Vaseline is a good thing to grow hair on a place that has been rubbed, or the skin just cut.

Fresh horse manure is the best and quickest (if not the pleasantest) thing to clean steel with.

If your little stick has one end thicker than the other, or a handle or knob, don't hold it by this end, but by the other, allowing about six inches to protrude through the hand, and your wrists and hands being properly placed (see Mouthing), this will bring the stick into the correct position.

Cobwebs. Leave the cobwebs in the roof of your stable, they are healthy and catch flies. If you have an accident and cut yourself, or horse, a handful of cobwebs will stop the bleeding quicker than anything, if you have no dressing at hand.

Accustom your horse to the company of dogs, it gets him quiet and handy, and does away with the chance of his kicking hounds, which makes one so unbeloved of the Master, i.e., take your terrier dog when hacking.

Never catch hold of the horse by the nostrils; a horse does not breathe through his mouth, except *in extremis*.

A horse cannot vomit.

And now, my reader, I hope you have picked up some helpful little things from this book; if you have not, do not blame me, I did not ask you to read it. What I have written in the foregoing chapters is the result of actual experience, everything has been practised and proved, and I pass them on for what they are worth.

INDEX

	PAGE
FOREWORD	9
ACCEPTING the Verdict when showing	97
Action and Manners—Showing	89
Action of Reins	17
Age of Horse	112
Architecture of Stabling	70
BACKING a Colt	54
Backing and Riding a Colt, and Re-training Horses	53
Banbury Bit	39
Bits—	
Mouthing Bits	29
Banbury	39
Pelham	39
Rugby	39
Sefton	40
India-rubber	41
Buying	45
Bitting, Reflections on	36
Breaking and Training up to Three years old	47
Breeches	117
Bridles	85
Bridlewise	60
Buying Bits	45
Brow Band	87
Buying a Horse—Some things to remember	107
CANTERING Hacks, when showing	94
Check Rein	16
Child's First Pony	100
Child's Pony, Feeding and Exercising	101
Child's Pony, Choosing a	104
Children's Ponies	99
Children, When teaching	102

	PAGE
Cleaning Saddlery	72
Clothing, How to remove horse	71
Coat and Waistcoat	119
Colt, Backing a	54
Colt, Putting Roller on	50
Command, Words of	20
Commencing Operations	19
Confidence, Gaining the Horse's	25
Continuations	118
Cord Reins	16
Curb Bridle, Action of	27
Curb Chain	86
Curb Chains, Attaching two or more	29
Curb Chains for Mouthing	28
Curb Chain on Pelham	40
Curb Straps	86
DISMOUNTING, Teaching to Stand Still whilst	62
Double Bridle	38
"Dressing" the Horse for Showing	90
EARLY Training	56
Education of a Four-year-old	53
Examining a Horse when buying—	
Begin at the Ground	108
Fore Legs	108
Knees and Splints	108
Hind Legs and Curb	109
Spavins and Thoroughpins	109
General Appearance	109
Back Rib to Hip	110
Cavity under Tail	110
Pace and Action	111
Height	112
Age	112
See Saddle put on	113
Weak Back	113
See Horse ridden	113
Mount and Try Horse yourself	114
Price	115

INDEX

	PAGE
Epsom Salts	76
Equipment for showing	98
Etiquette in the Show Ring	95
Exercise—Showing	90
Eyelashes	79
FEEDING	75
Feeding Foals	75
Feeding and Exercising Child's Pony	101
Feet, Care of Horses'	78
First Pony, The Child's	100
Fitting the Saddle	81
Flexing Neck Muscles	58
Foal, Teaching to Back	49
Foal, Teaching to Lead	48
Forage	76
Fore Feet, Movement of, in training	59
Four-year-old, Education of a	53
Free Riding in teaching Children	103
GAGS	42
Galloping Hunters when showing	93
Girths	82
Girl's Riding Astride	105
Girth Tabs	82
Green Food	78
Gymnastics, for Children	102
HACKS, Cantering when showing	94
Hacks, Trotting when Showing	92
Handling Foal	48
Hands, Position of	27
Hanoverian or Running Rein	41
Head Collars	71
Head Collar, Method of attaching Chain	29
Head Gear	119
Hind Feet, Movement of, in training	59
Horse buying—Know what you want	107
Horse, When Buying—Things to remember	107

HORSE KNOWLEDGE

	PAGE
Horse Clothing—and how to remove	71
Horse's Confidence, Gaining the	25
Horse—Conformation and Type	107
Horse, " Dressing " for Show	90
Horse hanging head—How to deal with	32
Horse, The " One-Way "	65
Horse's Feet, Attention to	78
Horse with One-sided Mouth	65
Horses, Re-training of	53
Human Voice and Training	20
Hunters, Galloping when showing	93
Hygiene	69
IF you become a Judge	97
India-rubber Bits	41
Inspecting Saddlery	66
JUDGE or Steward, Signals from, when showing	94
Judge, If you become a	97
KIT, Riding	116
Knee Caps	22
Know what you want when buying a horse	107
LEG, To answer to	61
Leg and Foot Wear	118
Lip Strap	42, 87
Long Rein Driving	15
Loosing the Horse	23
MANAGEMENT—The Master's Eye	68
Manners and Action—Showing	89
Martingales	84
Method of dealing with Horse who hangs his head	32
Miscellaneous Do's and Dont's—	
Horse in stall, turn him round before girthing up	121
A cold backed horse	121
Don't leave horse in loose box with saddle on	121
After a horse comes in	121
When leaving the stable	121

INDEX

Miscellaneous Do's and Dont's—*continued*.

	PAGE
A sweating horse	121
Cold sweating horse	122
Ears—dry and warm	122
Never sit on, when you should jump off	122
Go in front and let him follow	122
Boxing a difficult horse, on rail	122
Horses by rail	123
Don't jerk your horse's mouth	123
Foundation of good hands	123
When training, accustom horse to whip or stick	123
Music hath charms	123
Always learning	124
When out hacking	124
A "dickey" tendon	124
A wonderful brushing boot	124
Two Secrets :	
How to deal with a filled tendon	125
Lotion for bringing down lumps or bumps	125
For cuts or abrasions	125
The horse's vulnerable skin	125
Clipping out a horse's ears	125
Turning out horses to grass	126
To get rid of lice	126
Girthing your horse	126
Tightening your girths when in the saddle	127
Stirrup leathers—don't cut	127
Vaseline to grow hair	127
To clean steel	127
How to hold the stick	127
Cobwebs and their uses	127
Accustom horse to dogs	128
Horse cannot Vomit	128
The horse's nostrils	128
Moss Litter	70
Mounting, Teaching to Stand Still whilst	62
Mouth, One-sided, How to deal with	42
Mouths, Re-making	31

	PAGE
Mouthing	26
Mouthing Bits	29
Mouthing the Colt	28
Mouthing, Curb Chains for	28
Mouthing Two or Three-year-olds	30, 51
Movement of Fore feet, in training	59
Movement of Hind feet, in training	59
Muscles, Flexing Neck	58
NECK Wear	119
Nose Band	86
Nose Band, String Inside	29
ONE-SIDED Mouth, Horse with	42, 65
"One Way" Horse, The	65
PELHAM Bit	39
Pelham, Curb Chain on	40
Perfect Mouth, Secret of	17
Pillar Reins	34
Points of a Show Horse	88
Pony, Choosing a Child's	104
Position of Hands	27
Progressive Education for Children	103
Punishment	64
RACK Chain	72
Reins—	
Long Driving	15
Web	15
Cord	16
Check	16
Action of	17
Pillar	34
Hanoverian or Running	41
Rein Round Quarters	19
Reins, How to hold when Schooling	60
Reining Back	62
Re-making Mouths	31
Re-training of Horses	53

INDEX

	PAGE
Riding, when Showing	91
Riding Kit—How to Dress	116
Rock Salt	78
Roller, putting on Colt	50
Rugby Bit	39
Running "in hand" when showing	97
Running Martingale	84
SADDLE, The	81
Saddle, Fitting the	81
Saddlery	81
Saddlery, Inspection of	66
Saddlery for Showing	91
"Saddles off" when showing	96
Saddling	54
Secret of Perfect Mouth	17
Sefton Bit	40
Shetland Ponies	102
Show Equipment	98
Showing Hacks, Trotting	92
Show Horse, Exercising a	90
Show Horse, Points of a	88
Show Riding	91
Show Ring Etiquette	95
Show Saddlery	91
Showing	88
Showing—Running "in hand"	97
Showing—"Saddles off"	96
Showing—Watch the Judge and Steward	94
Side Saddle or Cross Saddle	105
Snaffles	37
Snaffle, Action of Plain	36
Sore Nose	22
Spurs	119
Stable Hygiene	69
Stable Management	68
Stable, Planning a	70
Stable, Ventilation of	71
Stick, Changing from Hand to Hand	65

	PAGE
Stirrups	84
Stirrups, Altering when mounted	83
Stirrup Leathers	83
Straight Driving	22
Strawing	70
String over Check	32
Sugar	78
TEACHING the Child	102
Teaching Children—Free Riding	103
Teaching Children—Progressive Education	103
Teaching Children—Value of Gymnastics	102
Teaching Children—The Wrong Pony	99
Teaching a foal to back	49
Teaching a foal to lead	48
Teaching to answer to Leg	61
"The Passage"	24, 62
Tobacco, Use of	77
Three-year-old, Mouthing a	51
Tongue over Bit	44
Training Foals—Begin with Brood Mare	47
Training Two-year-olds	50
Training Yearlings	49
Trotting, Showing Hacks	92
Twitch—An Iniquitous Thing	79
Twitch, Substitute for	79
Two-year-old, Mouthing a	51
Two-year-olds, Training	50
USE of Inner Tyre Tubes	41, 124
VENTILATION	71
Verdict, How to accept—when showing	97
Voice and Training, The	20
WATER, Constant supply of	72
Water and Watering	72
Watering Hunters and Tired Horses	73
Web Reins	15
Words of Command	20
Wrong Method in teaching Children	99
YEARLINGS, Training	49